FIRST AMONG SUFIS

FIRST AMONG SUFIS

The Life and Thought of Rabia al-Adawiyya,
the Woman Saint of Basra

by
WIDAD EL SAKKAKINI

Translated by
Dr Nabil Safwat

Introduction by
Doris Lessing

THE OCTAGON PRESS
LONDON

Original title:
Al Ashqa Al Mutasawwifa
(The Sufi Lover)
by Widad Al Sakkakini
Translated by Nabil Fethi Safwat, MA, PhD
Edited by Daphne Vanrenen

ISBN: 90086045 6

Printed in Great Britain at
The Camelot Press Ltd, Southampton

'I shall tell her story . . .
and today I come, the last of the searchers,
not to dispel this precious memory,
not to clutch on a handful of sand,
but to release long-hidden pages in the East and West.
I stretch out with loving hand to gather them together,
as they do the mementoes of a Heroine fallen in the struggle,
so as to enshrine them in a worthy place.'

CONTENTS

INTRODUCTION

Jalaluddin Rumi, the great Sufi, said of Attar: 'Attar has traversed the seven cities of love, and we have reached only a single street.'

It was Attar who said of Rabia that she was 'a second Mary and a spotless woman'.

Contemplating such a claim, by such an authority, makes comment about Rabia difficult indeed. Rabia seems infinitely far away from us: excellence like hers is not to be comprehended by ordinary people; we can only acknowledge that excellence beyond our comprehension exists.

She is far away, too, in time: she lived through the end of the 8th century and a good part of the 9th (Christian Calendar). And in place: the civilization she was part of is not easy for westerners to enter imaginatively. It must be hard enough, by now, even for people from Islamic cultures.

She was born in Basra, at the time of that city's greatness, of a pious family, in a slum. Orphaned as a child, she was kidnapped, then sold for six silver pieces; and lived as a slave until her master, seeing in her – so we are told – the signs of saintliness, freed her. Thereafter she lived in extreme poverty, in the company of other mystics, seeking God.

In fact, little is known about her. Inevitably, when we in the West think about Rabia, we have to do it in terms of what we know of Christian mystics, particularly the women, Teresa of Avila and others. There are recognizable parallels. She passed through the conventional terrors and raptures that are familiar to us from them. The words she used, the prayers, the beseechings, the language of yearning love: this phase of her life – for it was a phase – is within our grasp because we have read it all before, not least because contemporary psychology has illuminated some of these attitudes, often from the point of view of frustrated sexuality.

But then something happened, and Rabia changed. She

became someone who was very far from what we know from Christian mysticism, or ecstatogenic cults in India and elsewhere. Suddenly – or so it seems to us now – she left behind a territory familiar to us at least by description, for the unknown.

Perhaps the question we should ask is: 'What was Rabia's quality, what was innate in her, that enabled her to go through the stages of the mystic search, like Teresa and others, both male and female, transcend them, and then enter a state which it seems they did not know? For they laboured and suffered and renounced, and subjected themselves to the extremes of asceticism, as she did – but she went beyond all the craving and the begging and beseeching; all the 'please give me', the 'I want, I want, I must have'.

What is interesting is that she did have to go through this phase. She was not the only Sufi to have said that certain attitudes are spiritual childishness. But Rabia walked this particular Path, and perhaps it was because she chose, or was chosen, to do it, so as to show us all that babyishness can be left behind.

She insisted on the primacy of love in Sufism, that Sufism *is* Love, but she did not mean it in the ecstatic pining sense; and she was the first to say that fear and hope, the twin staples of religion as understood by most people, were unworthy and secondary methods which could not yield the paradise which was their aim. She was the first: then others developed the theme. There is more than a hint here of Sufi attitudes towards evolution, and how teachings must grow with the need for them.

Prayer was not to be considered as a means of obtaining benefits. 'If God knows of my poverty, then what need have I to remind him of it?' she asked, when someone suggested she should pray for sustenance.

She understood the confusion between container and content which we still find in religion everywhere: when people spoke of the Holy Kaaba in Mecca, she replied, 'It is the Lord of the House whom I need. What business have I with the house itself?'

And she is reported to have been seen going along the street with a lighted torch. When asked why, she said she was going to burn down the Kaaba.

2

It can be imagined how such remarks infuriated the bigots who, alas, are always with us, and who, because of the state of Islam in that city, at that time, were particularly plentiful. One is reminded of Muhammed's: 'My back has been broken by pious fools.'

Seen hurrying along with a blazing brand and a bucket of water, and asked what she was doing, she said, 'I am going to quench the fires of Hell and burn Heaven, so that both these barriers to understanding shall vanish from the eyes of pilgrims, so that they may seek Truth without hope or fear.'

She sent the great Sufi Hasan of Basra three things: a lump of wax, a needle, and a hair. These signified, 'Be like the wax, illuminate without burning yourself; be like the needle, work without possessions; when you do this a thousand years pass as lightly as a hair.'

What she was doing was to use 'the illustrative teaching method', later highly developed by poets and teachers who came after her. It was unfamiliar to the sanctimonious and morbidly self-flagellating who surrounded her in Basra. Misunderstanding of it has caused Rabia to be seen in a bad light – then and ever since. But this is true of all Sufis who use it; and is the source of a great deal of the unsympathetic or baffled accounts of Sufi teachers. This teaching method takes no account of 'making a good impression' either on the people being taught or on possible bystanders, who almost invariably become confused: making a good impression, that is, in the sense of causing admiration. What counts is the real impression, in the Sufi sense; that the person or people involved learn what they should at a given time. It is helpful, in trying to understand incidents that seem bizarre, to recreate them as far as possible – to imagine, for instance, Hasan sitting there by himself with a lump of wax, a needle, the hair, thinking and thinking, until suddenly there was the moment of truth, and of a kind that would not have been possible without going through the whole process.

Stories about Rabia tend to illustrate the character of the persons telling them. They may describe, not the society Rabia lived in, necessarily, but the assumptions and biases of the societies the authors live in. Thus, this author is inclined to explain certain possible attitudes of Rabia by some that are familiar to us, and particularly to women of our time, preoccupied with ideas of self-definition. But it is a sign of Rabia's greatness, her power to enliven us, that one does wonder: What would she think of this and that phenomenon if she were alive now? If I had been alive then, what would I have thought of Rabia? But all this is to be expected when there are so few facts. Sometimes Rabia, and similar people, seem like those tests set in hospitals to determine the disposition of patients: shapes and lumps, and blobs of colour are shown, and the sufferer is asked to say what these remind him or her of: the diagnosis is made accordingly.

There is a large body of writing about Rabia, and by definition it is nearly all speculative. This new book by Madame El Sakkakini (a major contemporary novelist and scholar) is an impressionistic account of her life and influence, an extraordinary kaleidoscope of myth and reality, of imagination and fact. Among these strands we can find breathless reports of miracles; the venom of the cleric who feels belittled by an aim higher than his own; the anti-feminine bitterness of the fanatics – and some remarkable principles of mysticism and psychology incontestably originating with Rabia herself.

It is a book that must interest anyone who has wondered about this great woman, of whom so few and such tantalizing glimpses remain. It is easy to put oneself into the position of Madame El Sakkakini, faced with such a task, and with so little material, and so much admiration and love for her subject.

When you start brooding about Rabia, trying not to be overawed by her, which it is all too easy to be, then how rewarding it is. It seems that a particular quality of hers was to be able to turn bad into good. She was very poor at a time when Islam had become splendid, and when the rich disregarded the poor. She was a non-Arab when Arabs had become proud and despised people other than themselves. She was a woman, and at a disadvantage. Is it not of importance that a woman of such stature and independence of mind existed so early in the story of Islam, to show what women could be, and how they could be regarded? She lived surrounded by people who had turned religion into a way of emotional self-indulgence. For some reason Islam was expressing itself, then, in Basra, by the creation of numbers of fanatical ascetics who had forgotten Muhammad's: 'There shall be no monkery in Islam.' Had forgotten that he had chosen to exemplify the ordinary life, lived among temptations, without extremes, without inviting the dangers of sado-masochism by indulging in self-inflicted sufferings. These were her companions: yet she had to go beyond them to find her own balance. It could not have been easy to do. She was the lowest of the low – and yet she was the teacher of great mystics. There are anecdotes of her correcting and instructing Hasan, who was called the Teacher of the Age.

How much one would like to have actually seen her, this woman who survived such hardship, who was as much reviled and persecuted as she was loved and followed. It is tempting to try and recreate her, a solitary, lean figure, wrapped in her single dust-coloured garment, sitting on a brick outside the brick hut that was her home, silent in contemplation in the hot glare of the light that beat on the hovels of this poor quarter of Basra. But then you realize that this image comes from early imaginings about Jesus, perhaps a print or an illustration in a child's book you have forgotten – comes from our own tradition; and while it is a happy thing that there can be this link, these are only imaginings, and in any case it is what Rabia had within her, what she really was, that we should aim to understand and contemplate.

But how very attractive must have been her personality, for there survives in the terse accounts of the authentic traditions about her, some of no more than a few words, a dry wit, an originality, something salty and simple.

'I will not serve God, like a labourer, in expectation of my wages,' she said.

Asked whether she hated Satan, she said she did not. 'I love God, but I do not hate Satan. Love leaves no room for anything else in the heart.'

She held miracles in contempt, though she was supposed to be surrounded by them, following the Sufi principle that such things are a 'spin-off' from mere by-products of some other attainment or activity, not central to human development; when they are not falsifications and imaginings. Sufis are supposed to conceal their miracles. On one occasion, when someone was cooking a stew on the open-air hearth beside her dwelling, and she needed an onion, one fell from the sky. The other woman said it was a miracle from God. Rabia said,

5

'My Lord is not an onion merchant.' Interestingly enough, one chronicler writes that the onion was dropped coincidentally by a bird passing overhead.

And she was no milk-and-water saint. When a certain religious man criticized her, saying 'Women do not claim to be saints!', she said, 'And, unlike men, women do not claim to be God, either!'

All these great originators, exemplars, teachers, however simple and human and ordinary and straightforward they are in outward appearance, and in how they organize their daily lives, soon attract to themselves clouds of legend and gossip. Truth has to disappear into fiction. In which, however, there do remain small glimpses of the reality. The strength and power of these sayings of Rabia transcend all the things that were, and are, said about her.

'Oh Lord!
If I worship you from fear of hell, cast me into hell.
If I worship you from desire of paradise, deny me paradise.'

Rabia al-Adawiyya, this woman who was born so humbly, who lived as it were in the dust, who died seeing herself as of no account, has been regarded ever since as first among the Sufis, teacher of some of the most revered sages, one of the greatest human beings who ever lived.

DORIS LESSING

I

THE STAR OF RABIA

The greatest legends are those which most resemble the truth. Among such legends are the tales of stars which have appeared, flickering in the distant twilight, like eyes eternally contemplative and vigilant.

Such a star appeared in the skies of Basra in Iraq at the end of the 8th century AD. Its light penetrated the houses and the assemblies and burned there like a candelabra. It remained ablaze for nearly a hundred years: an unforgettable phenomenon, immortalized in the writings of men, in the speech of their tongues, and in the records of researchers from that time on.

If they had asked Rabia al-Adawiyya: 'Who are you, how did you come to be and how have you lived?' She would have answered: 'I was a star in the heavens, then became an idea on earth. I went about like the others, loved and hated, laughed and cried, erred and succeeded, until I was liberated and called no man master. I had transcended, annihilated my lesser self. Thus people saw me as an oddity, a stranger on this earth.'

So Rabia was born and lived: an abstainer, a Sufi and a lover. But not the kind of love that women are usually said to desire.

It was in the dark stillness of night that the labour pains attacked her poor mother. She had no one beside her except Ismail her husband, comforting and encouraging her, not knowing what to do; his pockets empty, her pains increasing in frequency and strength, pride and shame preventing him from calling on his neighbours for help. When she begged him to go and bring her what she needed to anoint herself and ease the pain, he was overcome with compassion: he had no alternative but to go begging his neighbours for some butter, and oil to re-light the lamp. He knocked on the door. There was no reply. Distraught and

7

bewildered, he returned. And when she saw his face, she wept.

But before long she had been overtaken by joy; she was safe and at peace. The cry of the newborn was shattering the stillness of the house and of that seemingly endless night.

Hearing it, Ismail hoped that this child would be a boy: his other three children were girls. But again, the fourth was a girl. He named her after her number – Rabia, the fourth. But few welcomed a girl-child: and yet 'God bestows males upon whom He wills.'

This attitude of sorrow over the birth of a girl had been inherited by men since the al-Jahiliyah period, the 'Age of Ignorance', up to the time Rabia was born – and, for some people, to this very day.

Rabia's father was no different: if it had not been for his piety and respect for his wife's feelings, he would not have hesitated to show his disappointment. As it was, he managed to contain his bitterness, pretending to be content with what God had given him, until the momentary gloom at his daughter's first cry had left his expressive face. He was soon brought back to the reality of life: the course of Nature cannot be gainsaid.

Rabia's father was no philosopher: he did not attempt to interpret the mystery of life, its snares, or what lies behind the existence of man. Sexual attraction, the feeling of affinity with another and the urge to marriage were not experiences he observed thoughtfully, as wise men do.

His understanding was simply synonymous with his belief in religious submission and the will of Fate. And – who could say? – perhaps the greatest Father and Creator of all had held in reserve for his daughter days of momentous history.

When a man is born, his parents will not know what his end may be. They may be proud or cast down, they may smile or weep; but from that moment on he is an unknown entity.

The days and years will unveil the pages of his life and his path. If every detail of our existence from birth to death were to be written down, it would fill volumes too dense for mortal eyes to read, too heavy for the hands to carry.

It is, however, believed of the Day of Resurrection and Requital that when each individual descends to his grave, he will be holding his or her own book of life, either in the right or the left hand.

I am looking at Rabia al-Adawiyya as if through eternity, or at the door of the infinite. In her right hand she is holding a thick book of pages without blemish, the first of which she is about to turn. She goes over it contemplatively and tenderly.

I shall tell the story of Rabia and what she may have been through of good and evil. Life is but a journey, short or long; and Rabia's journey was very long, hard and exhausting. She left at her passing a message echoing as a tree branch sighs in the wind. Our memories on this earth are like a heap of sand, lying still until blown away by a ravaging wind or scattered by a hand: they may settle somewhere, or be forever lost.

And so the winds have blown over the memory of Rabia, a memory touched by many investigators and students, some dispersing the sands and losing sight of Rabia, others placing her in some alien niche. And today I come as the last of the searchers, not to dispel this precious memory, not to clutch on a handful of sand, but to release long-hidden pages in the east and west. I stretch out with loving hand to gather them together, as they do the mementoes of a Heroine fallen in the struggle, so as to enshrine them in a worthy place.

From the night of her birth, events occurred in Rabia's life which were to shake the souls and bewilder the minds of men, causing sleepless nights to Arab and Orientalist alike, to Sufis folding back their long sleeves to dip their pens in inkwells as they concentrated their thoughts upon the being of this remarkable woman. Some saw her as an angel, some as a devil; yet others found the two opposites brought into harmony within her, the polarity of the extremes reconciled.

Rabia grew up in piety, austerity and chastity. Her father was an ascetic, a humble man; and in the practice of abstinence, of disdaining to ask for favours, of constancy in forbearance and devotion, it was in this atmosphere that Rabia grew.

Acutely aware of all that her father suffered in his destitution, she was withdrawn into herself as if graced with the gift of inner knowledge. She never asked for that which her peers asked. When food was served she would take a little of it, never hurrying to get another bite, but thanking God for his sustenance – in this way emulating her father. He was an

9

absent-minded man, often deep in religious dreams. Sometimes in a dream he would see the Prophet (peace be upon him); at another time he would be dreaming of the men and women of God. He would enter the house with no more than an old garment on his shoulders, covered with a ragged cloak. His wife would go about her poor home no differently dressed than her husband.

From her three sisters Rabia was to acquire the qualities of chastity, contentment and piety. Their verses of prayer would fill her ears, and she would join in their recitations and praise.

Early at sunrise she would awaken to the sound of her father's prayers as he recited them and made his supplications. She knew quite early in life what was *halal*, the permitted, the religiously licit, and what was *haram*, the forbidden.

The sayings of the righteous were always upon her tongue; she never reviled anyone, she never expressed discontent. Good manners were natural to her, and awareness; she was quick to absorb everything she heard of religious ideas and prayer.

One evening the family sat enjoying their dinner – all except Rabia, who would not eat, seeming uninterested in the food. Her father asked, 'What is the matter, Rabia, why are you not eating?' She answered sorrowfully, 'I do not know, Father, if this food is *halal*, lawful, admissible to eat, or . . .'

Her father was shocked at her reply, and asked her, 'Have you, O Rabia, seen us eat any food which was not licit, that you think that this may be so?' She answered, 'It is better to endure hunger in this life than to endure fire on the Day of Requital.' Had she perceived something untoward within the food?

Later that evening, as her mother cleared away the food remaining in the bowl, Ismail, still greatly surprised, pondered his daughter's answer. It seemed to have been given in words such as were uttered only in the circles of thinkers and holy men. He remembered hearing in the sermons of the Sheikh at the local Mosque that small children did sometimes develop spiritually earlier than others . . . as if maturing before their time. His surprise passed; but his joy at his daughter's spiritual inclination was enduring.

Each time she memorized a chapter of the Koran and recited it in front of him, speaking the verses with care, mindful and happy, the tears would fall upon his cheeks and he would say,

10

'Lord, for what have you prepared this girl? She is nothing like the others of her age . . .'

He often used to contemplate his daughter's behaviour sorrowfully, hearing from his Sheikhs that, for some ascetics and devotees, grief and darkness lay in store. As he watched her growing up so fast, her heart and her dedication all in prayer, it seemed to him that she was like people much older than herself.

One night he fell asleep as she was reciting the Koran; and when he awoke next morning he found her still reciting, exultantly, wrapped up, facing towards Mecca. She had her hands raised; then she put them to her face, as if she knew that Fate wished to prepare her in steadfastness and patience against the trials of the future.

Her father died soon after – and then her mother. And Rabia, still so very young, was to suffer much misery from then on.

She had lost the love and tenderness lavished upon her for so short a while. But she stood unflinching in the face of catastrophe, surviving by her faith and her abstemiousness: destitute, an orphan, looking absently at the vast world like a lost person seeking to be guided.

II

THE CITY OF BASRA

We can picture Basra at this time, at the peak of her development and glory. Inhabited by Arab conquerors, who not only took advantage of her potential political and geographical position, but also opened her doors wide to knowledge, civilization and religious studies, Basra was a well-built city, well endowed with mosques and institutions.

Her Great Mosque functioned like a small university, in this resembling the institutes of the 19th century, with its circles and methods of study. The learned were of two kinds, one group involved in linguistics and literature, the other dedicated to jurisprudence, the Traditions of the Prophet, and discourse. The inhabitants of Basra were also of two kinds: one rich and leisured, the other, very poor.

The population consisted of Arabs and Mawalis (non-Arab Muslims), Greeks and Persians. Rabia's house was one of those in the poor quarter, small and dilapidated, where the inhabitants lived from hand to mouth, their eyes, even as they lay in bed, fixed upon the luxury and abundance (and often arrogance) of the rich, which constantly confronted them. It was in this region that revolution and social upheaval had been foreseen by intelligent observers. Among the trouble-makers were the fanatics who had not benefited from education or religion. Alongside them lived the temperate ones, impervious to poverty or wealth, not caring for luxury or self-indulgence, who were no problem to the rich: it was only the discontented and the dissident who had to be watched.

Basra itself was never safe. It suffered disruption or calamity every other year: one year from political partisans, the next from religious rebels, the Kharijites; until the Umayyads, the Arabs of pure descent, at the first quarter of the 2nd century AH (after Hijra, the Pilgrimage Year) were at their wits' end over the disasters. To make matters worse,

12

Basra was struck one year by a terrible drought; and this once-blossoming city experienced a severe famine. The worst afflicted were the poor, among whom were Rabia and her sisters. They became down-and-outs, separated from one another in their search for scraps of bread on which to subsist: hunger is never merciful, it will not wait. It seized Rabia and her sisters, cruelly weakening them. Rabia was often forced to remain without food for days; and when she realized her sisters were gone, she knew not where, and she was left quite alone, she called upon her God to reunite her with them. It would be a long time before she saw them again.

As the hunger spread, opportunists and thieves appeared upon the scene, slave-traders capturing the poorest and most unprotected. Rabia was one such victim. She was followed and chased by a vicious thief, from whom she ran screaming and calling for help. She fell to the ground; he grabbed her like a despised object; and soon after she was sold to a wealthy merchant for six pieces of silver. She served her new owner obediently and in patient silence. This merchant was a hard-hearted man. He burdened Rabia with work, like a disgraced slave: he had no pity on her youth and sorrow. Whenever she managed to be alone in prayer, she would call upon her God, weeping and begging: 'My Lord, I am a troubled orphan, dragged down by the chains of slavery and injustice, and I am in despair. But my greatest anxiety is to know if you are pleased or displeased with me?'

She often imagined that she was hearing answers to her prayers and pleadings – messages of comfort and peace. As the days passed, she ceased to feel any burden of hardship or pain suffered in the service of her master. The solace she derived from calling upon God for forgiveness helped her to forget her misery and misfortune. One day she was sent on an errand to market. On the way back she was confronted once again by a vicious man, a human animal; and running from him, frightened and shocked, through the winding streets of Basra, she escaped – though with injury. She had fallen and broken her arm. She dragged herself back to her owner's house, lamenting and sorrowful. When she was able to enter into prayer, she addressed her God yet again: 'Lord, my arm is broken, and I am suffering slavery and pain; but I will bear the injustice. Are you pleased with me? Your pleasure, O

Lord, is my wish.' And such is the effect of pain upon the soul, that when the leg of the ascetic al-Zayynouni was broken he uttered no word of complaint. Rabia was cast in this mould. The interior horizons of the devout are so broad that they are able to make light of seemingly big events, and to bear pain more easily.

That night Rabia stood in prayer, with her arm bandaged to her chest, trying her best to contain the pain. Her heart torn by grief over her captivity and slavery, she called out to God to have mercy upon her and to untie her noose. Overhearing her prayers, her master realized that she was in great pain. He then caught the words: 'Oh Lord, you know that my heart wishes only to obey you, and that the light of my eyes is dedicated to serving you. Had my fate allowed it, I should never have stopped calling your name, not for one second. But you left me at the mercy of one of your cruel people.'

Her master, hearing this, was seized with awe and dread: Rabia's lament and supplication filled him with terror. He thought for a few moments, then came to a decision. As he looked towards her, he saw a great light shining over her head, illuminating her surroundings. He started up, calling Rabia, begging for her forgiveness, saying: 'You are a free woman, O Rabia! Remain with me if you wish. But if you prefer it, you can go, to live wherever you choose.'

No sooner had Rabia heard these welcome words of release than she thanked God, her heart filled with hope for the future. A miracle had happened, her broken arm was suddenly without pain, she could move it again, it was whole once more. Gratefully she turned her face to the rays of the sun, giving thanks to the Lord who had delivered her from the hardship which had been her companion since her parents' death. She sighed deeply, somewhat comforted. Looking at her hands, one free, one still captive in its sling, she saw that they resembled those of an old woman rather than a young girl: work-worn, neglected, calloused and abused. Who could say where her destination lay, now she was at last at liberty –and bewildered by that liberty?

She left her master when dawn broke, breathing deeply and calmly, slowly shaking off the effects of the eternity of slavery which had brought her to physical exhaustion.

14

I do not doubt that Rabia was like anyone who has long been shut up against their will and suddenly found the doors of freedom open wide to them. She would have been suspicious of what might befall her in the new-found world. Or she would have looked at it all with totally fresh eyes, like a person reborn. Everything would have taken on a different appearance; she would even have been distrustful of friends and relatives, fearing that the whole world was conspiring to force her back into bondage again.

None but a singing bird escaped from captivity could feel as Rabia felt, experiencing the delights of freedom, spreading its wings wide upon the air, conscious of being once more unconfined, landing on branch after branch. But we do not know where Rabia actually settled after her flight into freedom. Did she remain in Basra, which was after all the scene of her pain and sorrow from as far back as she could remember? Did she go to Kufa, where she knew no one? Or did she manage to reach Syria, across the desert? All this still lies hidden in history. No one has found out the truth, despite long and untiring research; nor have any documents been of help in the matter.

Basra had been her home and shelter, even though it had proved so cruel. She loved Basra; she knew well its roads and its paths, she was familiar with its awe-inspiring mosque and its crowded bazaars, she had lived among its assemblies of recitation, wisdom and religion. But was Rabia after her release really free? Was she able to rid herself of the memory of her first captor, who had used her as he willed? No one but the victim can really tell the after-effects of being violated and robbed of her chastity. That alone may have changed her approach to life completely.

It is said that sometimes the self finds protection against sudden emotional changes and upheavals through an inner mechanism – just as happens within nations and peoples generally. The human soul may be likened to a microcosm of nations where revolutions must inevitably take place. There exist in this world the oppressors and the misguided, who have long indulged in wrong-doing and then become repentant, asking for pardon and remaining on the right course; just as there exist the opposite. It can happen that in the heart of a dangerous criminal an idea of compassion and spiritual

sacrifice may suddenly unfold. How often, too, does temptation sway its hips at ascetics and abstainers – at those who,
prostrated before their books of religion, their beards prepost-
erously long, their garb of coarse woollen fabric monastic,
their white turbans upon their heads, come suddenly hastening
out from their cells and their devotion in quest of enticement
and seduction.

As I write this I am remembering the ancient history of
Bafnous the priest, wandering aimlessly out from Thebes in
central Egypt. He walked the desert barefoot until he reached
Alexandria in the north – where he prostrated himself before
the naked Thaïs. She and her court were intoxicated at the time
with wine and the odour of incense, her castle was humming
with licentiousness and dissipation; yet did she not become a
saint as she was being dragged to death?

There are strange reversals in this world, miraculous and
unexpected. This may have happened in Rabia's case, after her
sudden liberation. A great surge of excitement may have burst
through her, in a kind of revenge for the misery she had had to
endure. And if she did succumb, so young, from a need to
survive and a fear of struggle; if she did become tempted by the
pull of beauty and the promise of security and happiness, and
was indeed swept away by the stream which had carried off
many others like her, then no alternative would later have been
left her but self-analysis, reflection and assessment.

Alteration of the self is a natural phenomenon. None was
ever born who remained the same person until he died;
because life is like the earth itself, it has mountains and valleys,
and we travel upon its surface, high and low, none knowing
what his or her destiny may be. After her escape into the life of
liberated women, Rabia discovered a new kind of existence,
engulfed in nights of tenderness, far removed from the
austerity and chastity to which she had been accustomed. Was
she at all resentful of her freedom and changed circumstances,
since neither had helped protect her from further bondage and
lapses into error? Or was it that her insistence upon excessive
self-suppression, then her observance of the ascetic life, had
been so bewilderingly turned upside down? This is what people
have always had to face, regardless of race or religion.

How numerous are the pictures which crowd into my mind as
I write about Rabia during this time of change in her life.

16

Between her and myself lie twelve long centuries. The documents recording her story are spread around me. They direct and encourage me to search into what has previously been obscured in her affairs. As one's imagination travels great distances and explores deep questions, so do my mind and thoughts, streaming through the vast universe and the long years. I see the beautiful women, the wanderers and the young Thaïs. With all their seeming indifference to piety, and surrounded as they were by excesses of unrestrained licence, they were nevertheless inclined to sanctity. The Cypriot belle Manazidika asked that upon her gravestone should be inscribed the words: 'Here lies the most pious woman . . .' when in fact she had once been given over to a life of dissipation.

I move cautiously into this area, hoping that what I have not been able to find in the historical references, nor in the Sufi books, may ultimately become clear, and lead to certainty and truth. Some writers and researchers have long investigated Rabia's story, extracting it from numerous sources; but none so far has found any information that sheds light on this curious stage in her life. Others have tried to interpret the old narratives about Rabia's behaviour after her release, without recourse to anything except glimpses and hints into her early conduct. They lap all this up, either to slake their own thirsty imaginations or to support the bias of other opinions and arguments. Whether this was done for the sake of pure knowledge and truth or in order to cast aspersions and insinuations, I do not know. Historical accuracy should be regarded as a priority.

Questioning history is taboo: none should add to or subtract from it; and although the record of our past is not entirely safe from either tendency, owing to the prejudice and personal viewpoints of individual writers, nevertheless it remains well documented and supported by fact, and is traditionally regarded as sacred and authoritative. The historian does not have at his disposal the freedom of the literary man. The search for insight into Rabia's secret and the truth behind her life seems to call for an enlightening ray clear enough to help analyse and illuminate all this. And because we cannot find any document or fact to explain this period without distortion, the question remains unanswered.

No solid proof has been established to support the claim that Rabia went astray after her release and wanderings in the desert. She may have loved once and been disappointed: guarded guesswork, this, but a logical conclusion. The shock must have been severe; and even though Rabia had been given her liberty, though a Muslim who was not a full member by descent of an Arab tribe, she was still to be regarded as coming from the Mawalis – and so still was to feel the chains of servitude deep in her heart and soul. The imposition upon her of this inherited prejudice was most cruel; yet it was the custom among the Arabs of the time.

The position of the Mawalis in Arab life was based upon long-held traditions – especially during the time of the Umayyads, who greatly overplayed their role as Arabs of pure descent. The Umayyad policies were exaggeratedly based on the glorification of their ancestral heritage. This was especially true during the early victories of the Arab conquerors, which led to their seizing privileges not permitted to the Mawalis; and the latter eventually lost patience with all this discrimination. Out of this situation arose many problems, whose analysis, investigation and explanation has been the livelihood of many intellectuals. Early authorities have written numerous books on the subject. The Mawali issue was discussed by literary men and historians alike, past and contemporary because of its close relationship to the Arts and the development of thought, and the problems of loyalty and of being a Mawala. Among the Mawalis were poets and scientists who actually surpassed the pure-bred Arabs in aptitude, organization and speech. But the stigma of being a dependant embittered them; and this feeling, and their attitude to 'freedom', were complex hurdles they had to overcome. According to the information I have in my hands, it is possible to argue that Rabia's failure or disappointment in one of her love affairs could have been the cause of that remarkable reversal, that deep spiritual explosion, which was to change her whole life. She joined the ascetics in her community. She turned away from the influences of the world while still so very young, preferring the assembly of prayer and invocation to every other thing. We know of no one in history who has entered the ranks of the ascetics without previous strong cause. It is the more remarkable when, like

18

Rabia, the one concerned has maturity of thought, beauty, and a free choice.

Rabia's consciousness developed early. She was bright and intelligent, and had a capacity for deep understanding of religious matters. For this reason she was able to follow closely the learned ones of her time, unintimidated by the disadvantages of her sex. She received their knowledge as naturally as the men – and at times surpassing them in her grasp of the hidden mysteries and the minute details of jurisprudence and the meaning behind the discourses of the Prophet. She never missed anything from the religious instructional corpus. She memorised a great deal of the Hadith, the discourses and records of the life of the Prophet, which was considered basic knowledge for the student. In this kind of atmosphere lived a great number of thinkers and academics. They were divided between Basra, Rabia's city, and Kufa, both of which housed people esteemed in their specialities: in knowledge and science, and in life-style. Kufa was crowded with circles devoted to linguistics, discourses, jurisprudence and authorities on creed; also religious free-thinkers. The impact of these two centres upon other cities was great. Each of them was like a mobile school of thought and knowledge. Interwoven through them all was a body of opinion made up of many religious men who attacked the life of luxury, and the existing political and social structure around them. They had no desire but to please God. Ascetics, they would turn away from family and home and give themselves up fully to study and prayer. They would live a celibate and studious life, vigilant at night, fasting during the day. This common attitude had drawn these people together. They all had a sad and lost look to them. Their faces never knew cheerfulness, their lips never relaxed into a smile. They were full, many of them, of sarcasm and irony, and often spent long hours in continuous prayer and bitter crying; so that they came to be known as the Worshippers or Weepers. Among the most famous of them was Rabah son of Umar, and al-Qaysi, Sufian Thawri, Malik son of Dinar and al-Wahid son of Zayd. Rabia was the most notable of them all. She consecrated the nights of her life to prayer, calling upon God, sorrowful. If she happened to fall asleep for an instant, she would severely blame herself for that lost moment of wakefulness which had fled without her uttering the name of her Lord. After her evening prayer, she would go up onto the roof of her house and draw her mantle and head-scarf around her, saying: 'My Lord, the stars are shining, all eyes are closed in sleep, the kings have locked their doors fast. Each lover is now alone with his beloved, and so here too am I: in your hands I stand alone, in private with you.'

She would soon be engulfed in her prayer and remain so through the long night until daybreak. Then she would begin the recitation of the Koran until morning, renewing her plea thus: 'My Lord, the night has slipped away, morning has unveiled itself. All I desire is that you shall have accepted from me my prayer – or is it unaccepted? I was inspired to offer it, whatever your answer. Even if you were to drive me from your door, I should never leave it, the love I have in my heart for you is so great.'

Each time she woke she would be frightened and distressed, calling out to God to help her: 'All eyes are closed in sleep, the heedless lie apathetic, and Rabia, a sinner, is left in your hands. Your glance, your might and your loftiness forbid me to sleep. I will struggle against being overcome by drowsiness; I will serve you by day and by night, until the hour I meet you face to face.' Then she would turn to self-reproach, saying: 'Oh, soul! Why do you sleep so much? How many hours of the night you waste! Do you not know that the time will come when you sleep so long, you will waken only to the loud cry on the Day of Requital?'

The ascetics were dismayed to see the epidemic of levity and self-indulgence sweeping through Muslim life so soon after the doors of civilization had been opened wide to the people. Shamelessness prevailed and many had gone astray, not remembering God and his commandments. Others had turned away from the pursuit of spiritual progress, intoxicated by the lure of power and wealth. Yet others had inherited a long-standing resentment over the murder of the Caliph Uthman Ibn Affan. There was none to avenge his blood. This alone was sufficient cause for reaction against everything. These people preferred the ascetic existence, quiet and secure, impervious to the contagion sweeping the core of the Arab mind and their new-found life. Yet this extreme reaction has always been the result of internal as well

20

as external pressures. Ultimately it amounts to an escape from the reality of what is actually happening in life: its purpose is usually consolation for something lost or unattainable. Rare are those who choose renunciation for its own sake; and Rabia joined the Austere ones of her time to escape the harsh realities of her own existence.

She was embittered by fear and sorrow, and these feelings haunted her, however subtly. Anyone who studies the lives of ascetics will find that the cause behind their retreat from the world is very often psychological. Asceticism is seldom known to be inborn: the natural disposition of man is desire and greed. Therefore behind every ascetic rages a tumult, however deeply concealed this may be. The lack or loss of fortune, fame or a loved one: any of these may lead to a wish to forget and seek the comfort of serenity.

At the time of Rabia, asceticism was being preached by another native of Basra: Hasan al-Basri. His way was marked by an element of deep sorrow and despair. Tales of death, of the Day of Requital and the horror of hell were his preoccupation. He was terrified of the idea of the Judgment Day, which became the main topic of conversation between him and his companions. At first, he was socially ambitious; but his life ended in an atmosphere of harsh religiosity. He found in the search for knowledge, and the spiritual path, an abstemiousness of soul and uplifting detachment from all that, from the Arab custom of ancestral pride, had once ailed him. He renounced everything for the devotional life and the satisfaction of seeking knowledge, until his fame was unsurpassed in Basra. He became both popular and respected. When people talked about the art of jurisprudence and eloquence they said that Hasan al-Basri was its leader and its highway.

Prosperous Basra was the scene of his long life, which began in AD 642 and ended in AD 728. He was the teacher of the age. In his lifetime he taught several generations of students, and was especially renowned for a well-known school of religious thought which he established in Basra. The people who came to hear him were countless; and it is said that if all who heard him had followed him, the land would have been filled with recluses. But, as desiring the world is much easier than being indifferent to it, and the creed of the greedy has a greater and

21

more persistent number of adherents, many people soon left Hasan. Only the truly sincere remained. Their number, however, eventually increased as news of his mission spread. And after him it was the turn of Rabia al-Adawiyya to be the illuminating and the guiding star.

The discipline of Hasan was most widely manifested by a turning away from family and relatives, from the material side of life and an interest in earning a living. Celibacy was favoured above marriage; trust was reposed in God to provide sustenance and livelihood without work or effort on the part of the individual. At the same time the devotee would burden himself with intolerable mortifications, restraints and hardship – all of which was quite foreign to the true Islamic ideals and the Traditions and discourses of the Prophet. It was really a facet of a hidden inclination within the individual. The Prophet himself had observed the tendency of a few eminent Muslims to lead an ascetic life, and he forbade them to overdo this rigid and excessive self-denial. The pedants, however, and those skilled in narrow jurisprudence, interpreted the Koranic verses to fit their own view of the time, and as it pleased their own disposition and thoughts. They totally missed the essential point: that Islam is a religion of effort in the present as well as the ultimate worlds; a counsel of work towards the development of man and his well-being. The Prophet himself was an ordinary member of society. His life was a normal and a good life, lived in accordance with the Message, which was needed by humanity to emphasize in the first place the comfort of man, his growth and evolution – never his withdrawal and reclusion.

The members of this ascetic creed, who so severely mortified themselves, were men of science and learning, whether they came from East or West. The Arab nation, despite all the envy and animosity that surrounded it, was at the stage of rapid growth and fulfilment of its principal virtues. Asceticism was a heresy and an innovation paralysing to the soul: it lured heads into the noose, and then pulled tight the rope. Its followers had an inaccurate vision of 'good', which actually worked against all that they hoped to achieve – and against the fulfilment of those who followed in their footsteps.

Many deeds were attributed to them which they did not in fact do. And many foreign influences permeated their original movement, distorting the character and aims of its Orders. Asceticism was not something familiar to the early Muslims, whose religion had taken them out from darkness into the brilliance of day. This crippling influence was derived from early Christianity at the time of al-Jahilia (The Age of Ignorance), and from the impacts of the Sassanian and Indian cultures. Opinions have differed greatly as to the origins of this form of belief pervading the life of the ascetics. Researchers have looked in all directions, at one time pronouncing the source to be Indian, at others, Platonic; while some investigators have gone so far as to call it Magian, influenced by Zoroastrianism, which was in fact confined to northern Iran after the Islamic conquest.

How could these ascetics, whose inclinations had been turned by God towards knowledge, have so completely rejected life and criticised those who loved it? As the very ones whose hearts had been touched by light and who had worked their way so deeply into knowledge, surely they should have channelled their energy and effort into healing the epidemic of licence and bigotry spreading through the land, instead of arrogantly suppressing it? I do not know of any case where the followers of this school of thought tried to declare this openly, or risked confrontation with the ascetic tyrants by pointing out the dangers behind this deviation. The latter, it is true, were small in number; but they influenced multitudes of people with their narrow-minded mortifications. Today we are in a similar situation. But if we should happen to find among us a similar champion of asceticism and withdrawal from the world – however sincere – working for man's improvement and return to the right path, I wonder if we should praise his efforts, even though we have undergone such a great change in our general consciousness?

Those who took up the path of Hasan al-Basri may not necessarily have done so through confused thinking or hyprocrisy, but from a genuine desire to find God and change themselves, to the betterment of their circles of disciples and seekers after truth. It was a conviction, a light as it were in their souls, which lifted them above the things of this world. How often, upon hearing a knock at their doors, would they open them to find couriers bringing gifts to them, from kings: all this to induce them to join the world like others, and to seek the pleasure of the king. These emissaries would be asked to leave, sometimes courteously, sometimes with much indignation. It is reported that one such ascetic told the emissary: 'As long as I can find a scrap of bread such as I have here, that is all the beneficence I want.'

Rabia was one of the most extreme of these renouncers of wordly goods. She countered her natural feminine inclination towards refinement and leisure by abstaining from everything that the world had to offer, content to subsist on very little, and with only the most simple clothing to cover her body. The light of religion was for her the greatest substitute for all that women are usually attracted to. She stayed near the Elders of the Mosque; she held fast to Sufism and the observance of canon law. Closeness to God was her only diversion. Never caring for her youth, nor asking for anything, she gave all to prayer and devotion. The feeling of godliness overflowed in her, both in solitude and in company. She went all the way to seek the love of God, doing whatever made her feel closest to the Creator. Her devotion revolved around one thing only: completely renouncing the world and belittling it, while crying with fear and longing for the Judgment Day, constantly seeking forgiveness. When one day a man knocked on her door, proposing marriage, interrupting her prostrations before God, he was curtly refused and sent away. She never allowed any temptation to divert her from her great task. The Prince of Basra, Muhammed the son of Suliman al-Hashimi, when seeking marriage, asked who was the most worthy of women to marry; and he learnt, from the many recommendations made to him, that it was Rabia al-Adawiyya. So he presented himself to her, saying: 'I have an income of ten thousand dinars (gold pieces) a month; I will make it all yours.' She answered him in writing:

'Asceticism in this world is a comfort to the body and the mind. Desire brings sadness and pain. So prepare your provision-bag and make ready for your passing. Take charge of your own affairs, do not let others act as trustees of your Will so that they may soon divide your inheritance between them. Fast in this world, and make death your hour of breaking the fast. As for me, if God were to bestow upon me a fortune such as you have gained, or its multiple, it would not please me or divert me from seeking God for the twinkling of an eye. Farewell.'

24

Another mystic and well-known Sufi, Abd al-Wahid son of Zayd, asked for Rabia's hand in marriage. She avoided him for many days, outraged by his proposal; then refused him, reproaching him for his attempt to distract her from prayers and celibacy, reminding him that he was supposedly devout like herself. Being married, she explained, had all the potential of involving one with the joys and sorrows of the world.

This attitude of Rabia's towards marriage, and her harsh castigation of whoever asked her, was, from the ascetic point of view, consistent with the teachings of Hasan al-Basri. Hasan viewed marriage as a distraction from serious attention to religious duties, night-prayers and wakefulness, and one of his sayings was: 'If God wanted any one of his creatures to be blessed in this world, he would not occupy him with family and children.'

When Rabia was asked why she did not marry, she answered: 'There are three things that cause me to be saddened; if any man could relieve me of them I would marry.'

What were these three things, she was asked? She replied: 'First, if I died, would I be able to present my faith purely? Second, on the Day of Judgment, would I be able to present my Book of Deeds with my right hand? And finally, when the Day of Requital came and the righteous were to go to Heaven and the wicked to Hell, with which group would I be?'

The questioner could only reply: 'I do not know about any of the things you asked, God alone could ever know that.' To which Rabia answered: 'If that is the case, while I am so worried about these questions, how can I marry and fulfil the obligation?'

This was the kind of talk that came to be known of Rabia and her convictions. It is clear that she upheld what she believed in, and shunned everything that separated her from it and connected her in any way with the world.

Rabia chose celibacy in order to fulfil her reclusive needs and to go along with the companionship of other ascetics. She wanted to be alone with God and to transcend the inborn desires of the body. She felt her saintliness and innocence and sincerity to the degree that she did not wish to give an instant of effort to any other endeavour than that of pleasing God.

The belief of the ascetics beautified the idea of celibacy and freedom from the burdens of any occupation other than pleasing the Creator. The married person is in constant fear of being poor, is always having to save and collect; the celibate has no fear other than of God and the pain of the Day of Requital. Rabia and her companions gave themselves over to the loneliness of the recluse because they had found that the unreality of the world was the cause of so many misdeeds. But their fear of the Judgment Day, of the trial and punishment, in which they had become enmeshed through the influence of some alarmist interpreter of the Koranic verses and traditional sayings of the Prophet – all these were really causing them to deviate from the truth. They understood that the everlasting blessings of Judgment Day are bestowed only upon the struggling pious ones, while its obliterating fire awaits the self-indulgent and those heedless of the requirements of recitation.

The traditions about the ascetics before her used to reach Rabia. Fantastic tales were told about their deeds which contained more myth than truth. Some of the events had occurred at the time of the Prophet; but he had spoken against such distortion and separation from the world. It was he who said: 'Work in this life as if you are to be immortal; work for the future life as if you will die tomorrow.' The extremists, however, adopted only the second part of this renowned saying, and went to dreadful lengths in their self-torment, to cleanse themselves of their supposed sins, constantly asking forgiveness for imagined wrongdoings.

Among these was Bahlul son of Dhuayb. Clad in the traditional woollen garb, he handcuffed himself with iron chains behind his back, and reaching the summit of a mountain near the city, he looked up and cried out for help: 'Oh God, look upon your chained creature, who professes himself a sinner!' Another like Bahlul was Abu Libaba, who, regarding himself as a sinner and betrayer, chained himself to a pole in the mosque and stayed there until he felt that God had finally pardoned him. Yet others took vows of silence for days, and even years, as recompense for their misdeeds and in hope of remission. When the Caliph Abu Bakr al-Sidiq heard of all this behaviour, he condemned and forbade it, pronouncing such conduct to be a survival from the Age of Ignorance.

Yet there remained those who never ceased from praying in the mosque, and who never left it until their hearts spoke to them to do so, assuring them of absolution. Others walked barefoot as pilgrims, all the way to Mecca, begging God to bestow upon them his forgiveness and to accept and bless their pilgrimage. It is said that Ibrahim, son of Adham, spent forty years crossing the desert until he reached the Kaaba. Another similar one had himself led around the shrine of the Kaaba like a camel, from a ring fixed in his nose. This ascetic heresy was the cause of much censure and mockery. It was scorned by Islam, which had never decreed anything but a straightforward, good life for its believers, holding that God does not require anything from the individual beyond what he can do with his innate capacity and ability.

Yet the stories still come in from various sources and traditions, giving extraordinary accounts of the tortures these extreme ascetics put themselves through, in terror of the Judgment Day. They despised the world and feared its people. They wandered about the desert like madmen, finding refuge in caves or graveyards, begging forgiveness and crying from fear of God. They were idle, and wasted their lives. They would have done far better and been infinitely more useful if they had, for the sake of their God, worked as hard towards the betterment of life and society, and in the struggle for knowledge, rather than live in this useless manner.

A friend of Rabia's who held to the same beliefs and prayers as these other itinerant Weepers, was Rabah son of Omar al-Qaysi. He performed as it were an endless requiem; his eyes saw nothing but the morbidity of death. When asked why he was weeping so, he replied: 'Those with sins and misfortunes ought to cry . . .' He was often seen with an iron collar round his neck, upon which he would pull, crying out for forgiveness, until he collapsed unconscious.

Facts which have emerged from psychoanalytical studies on similarly conditioned men show that the ascetics had lost the point from which they had started, and towards which they were bound, both in this world and the next. They had, in other words, put themselves into a position where they believed that they were the *source* of action, with the whole world reacting to them: they never understood that they themselves were the reacting elements. They viewed this world as transitory, a

27

temporary halting-ground; and the coming world as ever-lasting. The material world was the way, the means, the key; the world to come was the destiny, the ideal. So the notion became fixed in their minds that they must sacrifice this world in order to gain the other. The greater the sacrifice, the greater the reward; therefore those who sacrificed the most were in fact the more greedy for rewards. The world shrank in their eyes and became a trivial thing.

All this can be traced from what these people said and did. Not even poetry escaped their morbid influence. Even the great poet Abu Nawas deferred to them in his famous couplet:

> If the world were judged by a man of penetrating mind,
> he would see her in truth an enemy, wrapped in a friendly cloak.

When the leading ascetic of his time, Abu al-Atahia, heard this poetic verse, he showed signs of being deeply moved. He said he would have given all the poetry he himself had written in his lifetime, to be able to claim this *one* verse as his own. Abu al-Atahia takes us, in his work, to the very heart of the lives of the ascetics, even though he was not one of them. Sorrowful love poetry was attributed to him at one stage of his life, when he joined the recluses, living in a cave. These caves were a refuge for all who fled the world. They served as a kind of monastery for prayers and pleas for forgiveness – if in fact they had any sins to be forgiven. Who in this world has lived his life without error? Even a look or a nod might cause annoyance and become a 'sin'.

The tolerant scope of Islamic teaching and real Sufi understanding did not permit this over-simplified reclusive attitude, this punishing of the self with hardship and fear. The great Prophet, as we have seen, participated in life and in the good it had to offer. The scriptures stressed that: 'There is no monkery in Islam.' And what was monkery but an intense aversion to marriage? The verses were clear in their portrayal of the suffering awaiting transgressors and the blasphemous; but if a person followed the right path and was a useful member of his community, he did not need chastising. The idea of eternal punishment was introduced in order to improve the behaviour of man in this world, and thus create

28

contentment within it. But some interpreters inverted the verses, crying out with alarm and picturing Earth as a paltry, wicked place. This false picture in turn confirmed the ascetics in their beliefs, and virtually paralysed them. Rabia was surrounded with this kind of talk, and it came to bind her in a way quite suited to her inclinations. She refused marriage, which was generally the most cherished aim among women. She went against her inborn nature, burying deep in her heart the longing for motherhood which is, again, felt by virtually every woman. Others who have done this have been accused of deviation and abnormality: of repudiating that for which they were partly created – the propagation of mankind. I do not doubt that Rabia, intelligent and religious as well as womanly, had curbed her feminine impulses. She had been gifted, not only with a natural comeliness, but with a spiritual desire that suited her austere nature and provided the means of fulfilling her other-worldly, ideal life. I believe that she kept her human desires locked deep within herself, lost the key and forgot what was locked away.

It appears to me, too, reading of conversations she had with her spiritual friend Rabah al-Qaysi, that when she saw him once kissing the child of one of his relatives and tenderly holding it close, she must have completely lost her maternal feelings. She was shocked to see her ascetic friend kissing the child, and said: 'May God's name be glorified, I did not think there was room left in your heart to love anyone but *Him*.'

When Rabah heard her rebuke, and understood what she meant by it, he was so hurt that he immediately fainted. When he came to himself again, wiping his brow, he said: 'Love is a blessing from God bestowed upon man in order that he may be kind to children . . .'

But what Rabia had intended by scolding the ascetic for bending to kiss the child so tenderly was to remind him that love for God ought never to be replaced by anything else, no matter what it was. An outpouring of love from the heart which was not directed towards God alone failed, as far as she was concerned, to fulfil the way of the ascetic. She had become like a barren land, she who had once been so full of life and passion. But that was before she had become so lost in the love of God that she could find no substitute for it in any man. The spirit of Islam rejected such coldness and harshness. If her attitude to Rabah and the child had come from a man it would have been bad enough: how much more unnatural coming from a woman!

But Rabia was not like other women. She chose to give her life to God, not man from whom she had experienced nothing but misery and enslavement. She longed for freedom more than she longed for love. So she used asceticism as a way to freedom – to avenge her past. Her steadfastness in this became so much part of her, that her feelings and her whole sense of judgment took on an altered perspective. Her eyes saw through a dark filter, as an impression is registered through the eyes of a monk. Nothing in her history indicates that she was ever prosperous, or knew the feel of smooth silk on her body. She wrapped herself in her rough Sufic mantle; slept on reed mats in her prayer-niche; and continued this way of life until the day she trusted her female attendant Abdah to wrap her in this very mantle on her death-bed. Looking back through the intervening generations, I can see how this immortal woman shone so brightly in an age so preoccupied with conquests, social matters and book-learning. It was the beginning of an era where women were opening up to the new life, happy with the beautiful commodities around them. But Rabia shunned it all, in spite of having repeatedly been offered many such things: she preferred what was, to her, something of more lasting and higher value. She did not associate with other women who were attracted to culture and the ways of society, or even perfectly natural things like sex. With that, she had nothing to do.

Every man and woman should be able to live in accordance with what suits him or her, without jeopardizing the well-being of others or infringing the law. Provided they do so, we have no right to come between a man and his freedom to act as he wishes. Rabia for her part was endowed with a consciousness, experience and faith seldom possessed by other women; she was never known to act rashly or heedlessly on any occasion. Nor was her asceticism a cause of annoyance or harm to anyone, even though asceticism itself is a departure from the norm, and from what is considered to be a socially balanced attitude. Yet it is often true that the imbalance of the thoughtful is much better than the conservatism of one who takes no thought.

III

THE TIME OF RABIA

Rabia lived during a spectacular Islamic era: the most vigorous period in Arab history, when the world had just been opened up before the people. The inflow of cultures from the surrounding countries was welcomed. Within these lands lived the Iranian Sassanians, the Indians, the Greeks and the Byzantines, who embraced Islam in great numbers. The Muslim conquest had spread in its wake the religious teachings, and this glory was shared among many countries including Iraq and Syria. Basra in Iraq was, as we have seen, the city where Rabia al-Adawiyya was born and where she lived until her death in AD 801, the 2nd century of Islam. This date is the one agreed upon by the majority of historical and Sufistic records. So it is incumbent upon us to learn about this good city which reared Rabia and saw her become matchless among women. She attained her unique position wholly through sincerity and trustworthiness, not in compensation for some weakness, or through pretence, or as if adopting some profession of faith.

Basra was built during the Caliphate of Umar Ibn al-Khatab, on the Persian Gulf. It was the port and emporium for all the boats and ships which came upstream from Baghdad and Persia, and also for the caravans arriving from the Arabian Peninsula. The town of Basra itself was built in the year AD 637, two years before the city of Kufa. A grand mosque was built, in the style of the new Islamic architecture, which was under the sponsorship of Ziyad Ibn Abyh of the Umayyads. Basra was the winter resort of Ziyad Ibn Abyh, Kufa the summer resort. Many Arab tribes and communities, among them the tribe of Bani Tamim, migrated to Basra, and enjoyed living there. Many from the desert, and from other parts, flocked into this city with its important geographical position. They all helped to build Basra.

31

Authoritative historical documents have shown that the tribe of Bani Tamim were people with a great passion for poetry, and also quite sophisticated critics. They never cared much for theorizing or debate, preferring to engage in discussing logic and grammatical syntax; nor were they interested in sensationalism or deviation from the regular use of language, as were the people of Kufa. They were of Sunni, orthodox Islamic, belief, and like many of their elders were followers of Sufism, and led an abstemious life. Among them were Hasan al-Basri, Malik Ibn Dinar, Fazl al-Raqashi, Abd al-Wahid son of Zayd, and Salih al-Mary.

As Islam spread, the Arab conquerors realized the potential military position of Basra, located in the centre of the conquered countries, with a convenient waterway to the coasts of Arabia, India and Persia. Soon, however, Basra began to develop into something different from what the early conquerors had planned. She became the meeting-ground for people from far and near alike; a busy centre of commerce, crowded with schools of science and religion, and the home of many scientists and men of knowledge, who discussed all kinds of learned subjects. Their discourses were based on the Koran and the Traditions of the Prophet, from which early Arab thought was derived. The latter had developed both from the Muslim observance of the teachings of the Koran and from the traditions of other nations, and it was presented through an unsurpassed use of fine language. So the earliest Arab books and assemblies of wisdom taught the basics of law and linguistics. Their endeavour was also to collect the Arab linguistic heritage from verse and poetry, and to determine the impact of this language.

Among the men of knowledge reared or residing in Basra, teaching the sciences of divine law, language or jurisprudence, were a select group of skilled and wise thinkers. A great school had been formed in Basra during Rabia's time, which had several major educational branches, and students from all round the country who had turned to Islam. It was characterised by a unique methodology, a certain new intellectual approach to society and literature becoming distinctive of Basra. At the same time, the Arab nation had begun to split up into different ethnic and political persuasions. Basra for the most part inclined towards the Sunnis, and

Kufa to the sect of Ali; Syria favoured the Umayyads, while the Kharijites migrated to the Arab Peninsula, on which they imposed their own character. These differing currents of opinion collided with one another, affecting thought and society as a whole. It was a clear picture of national partisanship between the Sunni, the Shi'i and the Zubairi sects; and the controversy between the Umayyads and the Kharijites finally ignited this sectarian hostility, arousing the people to rebellion and civil war. The history of the Arabs is full of disasters and calamities of that kind. The fact that Basra had, for example, formulated a different formal language and syntax from neighbouring Kufa, resulted in the historians holding conflicting opinions as to the true nature of Arabic grammar.

As this controversy became more heated, burning hatred and ill-will reached the stage where exaggerated fears about the fundamentals of religion itself grew widespread. And so emerged a general realization of the need for a dampening element in all this conflict. A new so-called al-Marjaa creed was founded. This aimed at halting the dispute until such time as the upheaval had subsided, and calm and thoughtful minds could be applied to the task of finding a balanced answer.

At the head of this powerful stream of thought coming out of Basra there stood, as it were, a wall deterring all other opinions from penetrating. This was in the person of Hasan of Basra. He was constantly struggling to keep out any non-Arabic opinions on the matter, which came from India or Persia and appeared like snakes at any opportune moment. His efforts left a lasting psychological impression for many generations to come.

These new dangers were mostly imagined phobias inherited from the diffusion of cultures; and although in due time all the trouble subsided, it had on one hand greatly benefited the range of art and civilization. No one can deny the wisdom of India, the craftsmanship of China or the knowledge of Persia: without them the Arabic civilisation would have ceased to develop and flourish. On the other hand, this wave of foreign cultures was new to the Arabs, and only excited antipathy in their folklore, festivities and songs.

Of the individuals belonging to the various schools, pursuits, and ethnic backgrounds in Basra, some were, as we have seen, of a highly civilized class, rich and influential, while others living next to them were extremely poor and resentful. It was a crowded city with nothing to unite it but the oneness of religion. The predominant cry here expressed the principle of Islamic teaching that, 'there is no difference between an Arab and a foreigner except in piety'. Among the non-native Muslims there were indeed men of goodness, great knowledge and devoutness; but the rulers and heads of state could not easily swallow what was to them 'that theory'. It came hard to some of them to be liberal towards the non-Arabs. The inherent nature of politics, however, was often short-circuited by this great teaching; and among the strangers who converted to Islam were men of prominence in thought and liberality. The Mawalis, the non-Arab Muslims, were among the most outspoken and indignant on the subject of these suppressed God-given rights. They used different means to achieve their aim of equality; but early on they realized that the best way of fulfilling this quest was to elevate themselves, through education and knowledge. Knowledge at that time meant jurisprudence, which was based on both the Koranic verses and the sayings of the Prophet. The social order in the home and in the community at large was derived from them. These teachings had to be interpreted coherently, with due regard for historical sequence, the actions and philosophy of the Prophet, and finally the stories of the lives of early prophets and of the four great Caliphs after Muhammed.

During the time of Rabia this knowledge was the one in which her own people, the Mawalis, particularly excelled. They led the intellectual streams during the rule of the Umayyad dynasty. They achieved this both in order to humble the superior attitude of the Arab extremists and surpass them in logic and awareness, and also to come closer to the ruling authorities. Their choking bitterness over that attitude, however, did not leave them without resentment and deceit. Neither did their inherited customs fail to influence the local religious doctrine, causing sectarianism which in turn increased the heat of the highly tense situation. Much superstitious nonsense, of which Islam was originally quite innocent, became painted with an Islamic coloration. Political, tribal and ethnic partisanship were responsible for the creation of strange groupings and sectarianism. There were vestiges of old religious beliefs like the Brahmin and Sabean. Weak-minded and irrational ideas about the transmigration of souls, dispensations, the hereditary rank of the Imams and other superstitions were all partly the result of the ill-will and vengeance of the Mawalis towards those who had belittled them. They continued to spread this venomous malice until the rule of the beneficent Caliph Umar Ibn Abd al-Aziz, who gave the Mawalis his protection and support. Not until then had they been able to breathe the air of freedom or truly hope for the justice that had so long been their quest. Abd al-Aziz had to face a great deal of opposition on their account, from contemptuous and ethnocentric critics; but the Mawalis found peace and comfort under him. He entrusted their wise men with posts in the judiciary and in jurisprudence. One such individual was Yazid Ibn Habib Mawla al-Azd, who combined excellence in discourse with a considerable religious knowledge and who was responsible for the recording of the historical sequence of the Islamic conquests. He was a Nubian Berber who died in AD 746.

Another Mawala of knowledge and sincerity who was cherished by the assemblies of wisdom and religion was Hasan al-Basri, who, as we have seen, had been so distressed by the corruption of Muslim life. After calling for justice and the improvement of living conditions for a long time, he withdrew into ascetic teaching until the end of his life. His students and followers took the torch from him, and he died, according to the ascetics, the Leader of the Epoch.

Rabia was present at the assemblies of his followers; she observed their recitations and joined in their studies, and continued to do so all her life. She eventually surpassed all her contemporaries in this persuasion which suited her nature so well. She observed the happenings of her time and knew fully the ramifications of the intellectual and social life around her. Nothing seems to have escaped her. Eventually she arrived at the spiritual belief which was of her own evolving, which freed her from man and allowed her to move toward God alone. She experienced a sense of calmness through this approach. To her, man was a great disappointment. She knew him only as an oppressor, unjust, never hesitating to subdue the world for his own satisfaction.

If we wish to sum up the background of Rabia's time we can say that she lived in the splendour of the Umayyad era, and during the rise of the Abbasids. This stage of Arab history was most eventful, with all that the kings did and built, and their endeavours towards preserving material and spiritual values. If only this period had been blessed by a calm and balanced political life, it could have brought together the glories of Arab flowering, the triumph of thought, and purity of attitude. But the ever-present fanaticism, bigotry, partisanship and great desire for power and high position, kept them from attaining fuller development. It almost seems now that these events were expressing the very nature of the Arab and Muslim peoples, as if these propensities were inherent, going back many generations; while the fundamentals of religion are innocent of such influences. These nations will never be able to return to their early glory unless they can rid themselves of these diseases through love and understanding. If they are to create an entirely new kind of citizen, they need the higher guidance of God and love for their country. This has to be achieved first: only thus can we fulfil the true message of religion.

IV

AMONG THE GOD-INTOXICATED MEN AND WOMEN

Rabia joined the circles of the pious and the strivers after God, this striving being understood by them in terms of night vigils and long hours of prayer. We know of her distress over her own lapses from wakefulness: the truth is that she became lost in the actions of prayer. She followed closely the example of her mentors, those devout men who, like herself, were disillusioned by the world and all that was in it. This wakefulness at night and fasting during the day was their way of coming closer to God and attempting to exist in an atmosphere free from evil.

When something drastic happens to man, the whole world for him becomes darkened: he wishes he had never been born. All sorts of past events become clear in his mind, and he grows so sad that he is unable to move, like one who is severely wounded. If this is so after a single shock, how much greater the sorrow must appear when it seems to be there to stay?

The pleading for forgiveness and the solemn praying were distinctive of those who had surrendered themselves to God and the final Judgment. Often they cried throughout the night, until their eyelids grew red and their foreheads became hardened from prostration upon the ground. Stories were told about these Weepers; many literary works were devoted solely to them and history gathered them into its immortal pages. They themselves wrote about what they said and did, how they thought and conversed with one another, and how they interested others in their way. Rabia was never without the companionship of such men. They influenced her and learned a great deal from her. They questioned her and received answers that sometimes satisfied and often shocked them. They debated with her so that she was able to unburden herself a little of the great thoughts within her brilliant mind, which she needed to share with others.

37

One of those who were most often present, and who joined Rabia in worship, was Sufian al-Thawri, who called her the Adept. One day he said to his brethren, 'Come, let us join our friend, for I am never at ease if a day passes without my listening to her.' When they had entered the house and came into her presence, Sufian raised his arms to heaven in prayer:

'Lord, I ask thee for safety . . .'

Hearing this, Rabia burst into tears.

'What,' asked Sufian, 'is the reason for this weeping?'

Rabia answered, avoiding his eyes: 'You are the reason; you caused me to weep. Did you not know that safety comes from leaving what is in the world? But you remain in it, and you are almost drowning . . .'

It seems that Sufian did not give himself wholly up to prayer as Rabia did. He was in the world for a short while, and spent this time preaching. And Rabia considered him among those too desirous of the world. She wanted him to give his fullest attention only to God and the Day of Requital.

Sufian al-Thawri once related this:

'I was with Rabia one night, and we prayed together until daybreak. In the morning, she said, "We ought to fast this day, in thankfulness to God for the prayers he allowed us to perform so long last night." '

Another of the ascetics told a story of how one night he started to worship with Rabia, and to reminisce about what God had bestowed upon them of knowledge and understanding about religious matters; and they talked long and went deep into the mysteries of existence, until this ascetic forgot that he was a man and she a woman. When they had finished talking, he felt that he was but a poor individual and she, so rich with knowledge and sincerity, wealthy indeed compared to him.

This thoughtful companion had no doubt opened himself to Rabia and discovered the vast distance between their two stages. She appeared to him as possessing the mind of a sound and unsurpassed man, both in her speech and spiritual understanding, all of this indicating a strong consciousness and deep, sound judgment.

Sitting in the company of Rabia, Sufian once said:

'How sad . . . !'

And Rabia, without letting him finish, replied:

'Do not lie! You should rather be saying how seldom we are honestly sad. If you were truly sad, you could not be content to live thus . . .'

She often asked her companion to renounce the world and give himself wholly to God. The thought of the Day of Judgment terrified her, and she constantly prayed and asked for deliverance from punishment.

Each time she heard the call to prayer she would imagine hearing the trumpet call on the Last Day. Whenever a swarm of locusts took off into the air, again she would think of that final day. Upon seeing snow, she would think of the pages of the Book of the Day of Judgment. All these associations of images have been described by psychologists. Upon seeing lines in the snow, for example, some people become highly excited, and all kinds of complexes become evident. Something may trigger off a submerged memory, overwhelming the individual with agitation. Surely the same applies to this fear of the horror and tortures of the damned: it could well be the cause of such exaggerated praying and entreaty.

Rabia was asked once by an enquirer:

'I have incurred a great deal of sin. If I repent, will God forgive me?'

She answered: 'No; but if *He* were to forgive you first, *then* you would be able to repent.'

She believed that man could not be granted forgiveness just because he chose to repent and ask for remission of his sins. One first had to struggle hard to win God's pleasure, by totally abstaining from wrongdoing. Otherwise, Rabia averred, the mere action of seeking forgiveness, without abstaining from that for which one is asking to be pardoned, is another form of human deceit. When the action of abstaining and that of asking for pardon do not coincide, how can there be forgiveness? Rabia uttered many paradoxical truths which invite scrutiny; like her observation that, 'The very fact of our asking for pardon calls for forgiveness in itself, because it lacks sincerity.'

Or this: 'May God forgive the total lack of sincerity in my plea, when I say, "God forgive me".'

All this severity about asking for pardon is clearly the sign of an unquestioning belief in the Day of Resurrection, requital, judgment and punishment. It also shows that those who became lost in the love of God had clear, transparent souls unable to cope with the problems of everyday life, let alone solve them; whereas the true religion had never suggested the separation of man from his normal day-to-day existence. To use a contemporary expression, I would call these people prayer specialists. But what Islam and the generous Prophet taught was the principle of doing what is needed in life.

Remorse is an exaggerated expression of regret, which may severely limit the capacities of the individual concerned. It is referred to by spiritual teachers and psychologists as an inner voice that impels the erring one to erase his wrongdoings through prayer, good deeds and obedience to God. To contemporary man, this voice is known as his conscience. And repentance is a kind of sincere passion affirming the desire to compensate, through compassion, for an evil deed, regardless of how great the wrongdoer's malice has been. He must return to a state of true regret, and acquire remission from God, the law, or his fellow man.

And Rabia, the ascetic with her nightly prayers, long implored God to forgive her and accept her repentance. I wonder, what was it that you were so importunately repenting, O Rabia? What offence did you commit?

I find no answer to this except a speculative or imaginative one. To explain or interpret the events that she went through, or to impose a charge upon her, would be impossible after all this time; and Rabia is unable to speak. I have not been given the power to see into the unknown; nor have I the Sufistic perception to look into her inner spiritual states. Of all our advanced instrumentation such as television or radar, nothing is able to return to us an instant of the past, so that we may discover the truth of what we cannot see for ourselves.

Although most of the recorded interchanges took place between Rabia and her ascetic brothers, she had many extraordinary conversations with her perplexed religious sisters as well.

They were remarkably intelligent. Like Rabia, they took the way of asceticism and adapted to this psychological state. Basra had attracted various women to this way, from jurisprudents to women interested in religion and law. There were other women, too, interested in politics and national- ism, and participating in the intellectual endeavours of the time. There were the singers, the lutenists, the wanton women and the idle ones.

But those who took to the way of Rabia, although they were not few or insignificant, could not persevere as she did. Nor were they gifted with her perception or depth or steadfastness in prayer. They could not comprehend the vastness of Rabia's intelligence, nor her way of connecting with the spirit of God and becoming immersed in the secrets of the Truth, and most of them soon developed signs of strange abnormalities. They were considered by certain other men and women as belonging to the 'creed with a touch of madness': so much so that Abu al-Qasim of Nishapur (who died early in the fifth century of Islam) wrote a book called *The Crazed Intelligents*. He mentions a group of these early women ascetics whose minds became possessed as a result of their carrying too far the prayers and separation from life. One such woman was Hayuna, a friend of Rabia. After spending a day with Rabia, she decided to stay overnight; and when they had passed a great portion of the night in continuous prayer, sleep began to weigh on Rabia's eyelids, and soon they were closed. Hayuna, sitting next to her, noticed this, and shook Rabia, saying: 'Wake up, Rabia! Now is the time for the wedding of the righteous, you who have adorned the brides of the night and made them shine with the light of dedication!'

Nishapuri related another incident about this ascetic woman friend of Rabia. Hayuna was out walking one day when she saw Abd al-Wahid son of Zayd, who had once proposed marriage to Rabia. She cried out, rebuking him: 'You talker, talk about yourself! By God, if you were to die, I would not walk behind your coffin . . .'

He asked her, 'And why is that, Hayuna?'

She answered: 'You talk too much about other people, and you seek to be close to them. You are like a schoolboy who memorizes a thing in the morning, but when he hastens to his mother's house in the evening, forgets what he has memorized; so he needs spanking. Go and spank yourself, Abd al-Wahid . . . spank yourself with the single-mindedness of the Adept, and refine yourself through abstemiousness. First make yourself the subject of your speech, and then talk about other people!'

When Abd al-Wahid heard this from Hayuna, he was so

41

mortified that his brow became drenched with sweat. He moved on, speechless, and spoke to nobody for a year.

It seems that Hayuna resembled Rabia in this respect: that whoever did not remove himself from the world as they did, keeping close only to God, she startled out of complacency with the kind of shock tactics often seen in Sufis. This technique, as the literature shows, was frequently misunderstood by bystanders – and still is . . .

They both forgot, according to literalists, that God had ordained that man should work for the general welfare of all, and that Islam specifically calls for orderly behaviour and a 'give and take' attitude in the world.

There were many gifted women like Hayuna: poetesses and jurisprudents well-versed in symbolic Sufi phraseology, who removed themselves from society in the manner described in Nishapuri's *The Crazed Intelligents*. Somehow Rabia was saved from this mental deviation. Her perseverance and resolution of mind were certainly equal to the greatest among men. She was in her time an example to womanhood of knowledge, sharp-mindedness and piety. She was counted by the Persian Sufi Farid al-Din al-Attar as being among the greatest thinkers of her era. He paid tribute to her in these words:

> If we have taken from Aisha, the mother of all believers, half of the Islamic religion, Rabia was not unequal to her; for she has given us deep insights, sincere dedication and knowledge. She is a phenomenon because she achieved what men could not achieve. She was the forerunner of them all. She had a spiritual belief that was strange. She developed it from the Sufistic basis of knowledge of her time. And this class of person existed on a high level of Sufism which could be attained only by the deeply perceptive, the pure of soul and the one most sincere in his religion. All these attributes existed in Rabia and placed her within that class of person, if she was not *the one* who started it all in the first place. In order to know the Idea of the Holy, one needs an undefiled heart, safe from imbalance and open to knowledge, so that the self may receive the living proof and feel the subtle truth that cannot be touched or seen as material things can.

In the tangled records, part legend, part hagiography, part

42

envy in their genesis, we find several strands relating to the various levels of understanding of the Pilgrimage to Mecca. Within this sparse but always fervent material we can see Rabia as religious enthusiast and then as Sufi; as well as learning much about the minds of those through whose writings we know of her . . .

V

RABIA MAKES THE PILGRIMAGE

It has been laid down that any person who can manage to make the Pilgrimage to Mecca should attempt to do so. Therefore it soon became a wish common to all Muslims, and the dream of the ascetics. Before our present age, which has so reduced the travelling time, by ship or by air, the pilgrims used to cross the desert on camels or on horseback. It was a long and exhausting journey, yet even to this day there are those who still prefer the traditional way of reaching Mecca. As soon as the Pilgrimage season begins, we find aspiring men and women full of hope and longing to share in the blessings of the journey. And when the moment arrives when the Kaaba becomes visible, their faces light up, they are smiling; for they have reached the land where God spoke to Muhammed, peace be upon him.

The overwhelming desire to fulfil this Pilgrimage became common to all Muslims who could afford the journey: the hardship along the way was never considered. The nature of caravan travel was hard both in summer and in winter, whether from punishing thirst or the stupefying heat of the sun. Yet these difficulties were in themselves an incentive to the pilgrims to realize their dream of reaching the House of the Lord.

As the years went by, it came to be accepted that the man setting out on the Pilgrimage was already lost. If he did succeed in returning safely, this was considered a great reward, and his whole family would celebrate this extra blessing of Baraka. The famous saying, 'The delights of recompense are in accordance with the trials and tribulations' (in other words, the greater the hardship, the sweeter the reward), was their consolation.

If this was the attitude of the ordinary people, how much more must the Pilgrimage have meant to the single-minded ascetics – and to Rabia al-Adawiyya, at the forefront of them all!

44

Many stories have been told about the tribulations of these men and women, some of them hard to believe. Nevertheless that burning desire to reach the Kaaba and the spot where the divine inspiration took place, did cause them often to go barefoot, to endure any hardship or sacrifice, and in many cases, death. Some died from the extreme conditions, others from attacks by gangs of thieves who set up ambushes to rob and kill them. Those who died were counted as martyrs, for to die on the Haj gives the Muslim that status.

From this vision of the distant past we see that the ascetics at the time of Rabia formed a large proportion of the Muslims who set out longingly to fulfil the Pilgrimage. They endured the discomforts and some took as long as two years to reach Mecca from Basra – impervious to danger, banditry or disease.

Rabia, the matron of the ascetics, made several journeys to the land of the Kaaba. She fulfilled the Pilgrimage, she fulfilled her dreams, travelling with the caravans in the desert, not caring about danger or illness on the way. At first, she used to chant and call out to her God as the convoy moved over the desert sands: 'My Lord, you promised rewards on two counts: the Pilgrimage, and the endurance of hardship. If my pilgrimage has not been right or acceptable to you, then woe is me: how great a calamity this is to me!'

This prayer indicates that it was spoken on the first of her pilgrimages, though history does not record the date on which she started her journey. It was her means of attempting closeness to God: not in order to gain merit, but to reach understanding of the truth and the secrets of the hidden world. She travelled to such heights in her consciousness that no wings could have taken her there. She extended her meditations, and formulated symbolic expressions in her speech and prayers – and in her actions and behaviour – that became a convention among a group of her ascetic brethren.

This stage in Rabia's development must have occurred after she was middle-aged, when she had matured and her perceptions had unfolded. It came naturally to her, beyond the level of religious conduct. Before that time, even if she had been taught by all the great Saints of the past, it would not have been possible for her to attain to the levels they, perhaps, had achieved. Nevertheless, advancement to the sufistic stages of Awareness and Spiritual Blessing (*kar-amat*), is not bound by length of time, nor by the efforts of the teacher and the taught.

A student may well reach with one tangential step, or in an intense prayer, a stage of awareness which has not been realized through many artificial disciplines. And it appears that the second stage of Rabia's long life of pilgrimage was in itself a Sufi pilgrimage, made for the sake of God alone: not in the hope of accumulating merit, or from fear of punishment; nor yet for any particular desire to enter the Holy Sanctuary.

Many incidents said to have occurred during this time have been attributed to Rabia al-Adawiyya – mostly of doubtful authority, although historical records have attested to the high state of blessedness in which Rabia lived. One story tells how she joined a caravan with her provisions carried on a donkey. Along the way the donkey died. Rabia stopped and refused to continue, saying to her companions: 'Go on without me. If my dependence had been upon you, I should not have taken this journey. My confidence is in God alone . . .'

She sat near her donkey, praying: 'My Lord, you invited me to visit your House. But my donkey has died on the way, and I am all alone in this wilderness . . .'

No sooner had she finished her prayer (according to Attar), than the donkey was up on its feet. She put her belongings on his back again and ran to catch up with the caravan.

Another such tale is related by Abu Ali al-Farmadhi, the teacher of al-Ghazzali. On one occasion when Rabia took to the desert to make the Pilgrimage, she spent seven years on the journey before she reached the Kaaba. The narrators may have told this story as an example of the inventiveness of the ascetics in torturing themselves with hardships.

Al-Attar, the author of *The Recital of the Saints*, added another legend indicating the blessedness of Rabia: that the Kaaba itself came to meet Rabia. Although I do not like to question this story, I believe that it has been wrongly told. These narrators tended to misunderstand Rabia's symbolic statements, through a shallow and superficial interpretation of them. This was a most dangerous common practice by which many a great man of knowledge, before and since Rabia, had his speech understood by its apparent rather than

46

its inner meaning. This surface comprehension of a sophisticated thought gave rise to a great deal of suspicion and resentfulness, and sometimes even to death for the speaker.

But for Rabia, as the significance of the Pilgrimage unfolded within her, it took on an altered meaning in her heart and her feelings; it came to embody ever higher aims, beyond the material. She longed for 'the face of God' alone. The act of pilgrimage became for her merely a physical exercise, performable by any living human Muslim. After her long immersion in Sufism she no longer found in herself the need for attachment to anything of this world. She no longer yearned for the Kaaba, nor cared for any traditional religious season. She ended her Pilgrimage with a purely symbolic utterance describing the Absolute, which is not bound by any time or place. But God is not limited even to that Absolute. Here we see the bravery of Rabia's voice, and of her deep conception of an Absolute of which she had never conceived before. It may well be that the long single-minded struggle and involvement in the search for God had taken her to that highly evolved state. She arrived at an understanding that prayer must be free of any desire for earthly attainments. If it did contain any such intention, it would be no better than selfishness or idol-worship. The ideal that can be touched and felt, and which has dimensions, is rejected by the follower of the True Way that knows no boundary or chains.

The history of Sufi thought, whether in religion or philosophy, contains many strange happenings attributed to people of high knowledge and learning who are then accused of speaking and acting in a manner seen by the ignorant and shallow only through its outward appearance. Such a saying, which is often attributed to Rabia as occurring at a time close to the season of al-Haj (the Pilgrimage), was:

I do not want the Kaaba, but the Lord of the Kaaba. Whatever can I do with the Kaaba? It is the most worshipped idol on earth. God has been neither within nor without its walls: he has no need of it.

This could have been devised by later detractors in order to create doubt. Invented variations were applied even to the Sayings of the Prophet Muhammed. Thousands of proverbs were contrived, fabricated and plagiarized. But what is

47

understood from these words of Rabia is that her whole heart and mind were dedicated to 'wanting the face of God alone'. Rabia pointed out the failing, common even in our day, of mistaking the container for the content.

What was revealed to her in her prayers came by virtue of her pure unwavering spiritual endeavour, and her effective not morbid, detachment from the world. The clarity and sincerity of her deep spiritual concentration yielded visions of a shining spirituality. She was no longer bound by the Pilgrimage to the House of the Lord and the land of inspiration. This was in accordance with the examples of former ascetics. But she knew how to make it at least partly comprehensible to us.

There were no longer any limits to her visions. The pressures of formal ceremonial laid no more restrictions upon her. She had, especially during her later pilgrimages, evolved into a new understanding of what lay behind ritual. So, during her discourse with fellow ascetics about the Pilgrimage, she used expressions which could be comprehended only by their inner purpose and meanings. But those who came after her, philosophers and interpreters alike, became confused by their own fanatical literalism. Among these was Ibn Taymia, who indulged in defamation of Rabia through his shallow outward understanding of her sayings.

We do not know exactly when Rabia ceased making her pilgrimages; or whether the reason was advancing age and physical weakness. Or was it due to an inner change – transforming her from ascetic into Sufi? It may have been this which led her to replace the dictates of intellect and superstition with the knowledge born of experience. Her unquenchable desire was to become absorbed into the celestial timelessness of eternal being: not to be limited, fossilized, walled in by time. All this became evident from her Sufic behaviour and illustrative speech. Was she in her unguarded, straightforward sincerity being drawn like a moth to the burning flame? We shall see how Sufism carried her upwards to the treasures of knowledge. Like one intoxicated, she no longer saw what others saw, but with a ray of vision untrammelled even by the artist's horizons, and not sensed by the body.

It was a faculty beyond sight and beyond thought. However hard and resolute one's efforts to attain to it, the height is beyond the strengh of any wings. How often has a chained captive, behind bars for long days and nights, held on to a single ray of light which reminded him of the blessings of freedom and thus restored his hopes? So with the visionaries and contemplatives who have flown beyond the obvious to touch the truth behind the existing world: however far off that be, they go back repeatedly to the ecstasy of search and submersion, asking for more.

VI

FROM AN ASCETIC INTO A SUFI

What appeals to me in literary and social studies is to follow the development of thought or the direction assumed by those we are studying. There is something extremely difficult in the nature of developmental processes. It is a hidden order that moves through the living matter. It is a process of growth unnoticed by the unaided eye. It is seen only through consecutive stages. There is not in all our scientific microscopy a capacity for measuring the inner processes of the unfolding of a rosebud. How often have we planted a small tree, and found to our wonder that it has burgeoned and grown without our detecting its development?

And so it is with Rabia, whom we came to know as a tender sapling, but who in a few years matured into a great fruit-laden, shade-giving tree. Within her shelter many a pious and forsaken one of the world has come to find comfort. But none has been able to taste or appreciate the delights of her fruit except those men and women of knowledge with the capacity to do so.

And this capacity in itself has degrees: none can attain to it except the people of clear vision.

The sensory and the incorporeal in Rabia came together as a piercing beam, revealing hidden secrets. She had no other aim left. She was fully drawn. No longer was she a mere night-worshipper, praying to God out of desire for his heaven or fear of his punishment. No longer did she weep in bewilderment through the hours of darkness, begging for mercy on the Day of Requital. She now had a different approach to her religious life.

The degrees of the enlightened are in a way similar to the degrees in our universities. The highest stage is reached when a man or woman of knowledge, after hard effort, has come to know the full truth. The process requires right effort, right time, place and associates.

Sufism is this higher stage, into which Rabia was absorbed through her clear vision, dedication and beneficence. And what was this Sufism which she reached after such prolonged asceticism and devotion, and in which she so totally believed?

If we were to attempt to define the meaning of the word, and to show its formal derivation, we should find that there are many definitions which overlap. It can be summarized by two schools of thought. First, some ascetics and religious devotees came to be called, or called themselves, 'Sufis' because of the coarse woollen mantle they wore. This was to distinguish themselves and their own abstemious ways from the wearers of the aristocratic dress of the time, as has been explained by the historian Ibn Khaldun, who linked the use of this mantle with certain aspects of monasticism and the early devotees. The Arabs, again, when calamity struck them, tended to wear coarse black wool, as al-Khansa did when lamenting her sons and brother. The second school of thought relates the Arabic word 'Sufi' to 'Safa' (purity), referring to those with pure vision; or to the word 'Sufa,' referring to the place in Arabia where certain poor Muslims used to find refuge outside a mosque. Yet another opinion favours the word 'Saf' (rank or class), because the Sufi is of the First Rank: he is counted as among the Saints of God whose purified hearts and liberated souls have been emptied of desire. But the Arabic language does not permit this kind of derivation and explanation; nor does it really serve to formulate the word 'Sufi', even if we reversed some of the successions of letters. The word 'Sufi', like the Sufis themselves, defies external inspection.

But the doctrinal definition of Sufism has numerous versions, both in defining its methods and branches, and grammatically, with respect to its external meaning and its intended underlying significance. So anyone who was a 'Sufi' explained and defined the term in accordance with his own attitude and understanding; and whether he was teaching or expounding. Anyone who investigated Sufism, or wrote about it, said only what he personally thought it to be; and among such versions was a major 'Sufi' book of definitions written by Abu Naim al-Isfahani (who died in AD 951), under the title *The Decorum of Saints and the Ranks of the Pure*. This author listed the definitions of the term 'Sufi' in accordance with the rhyming of words and the fads of the time. One such definition was: 'To be a Sufi is to flee from the Apparent into Being.' Another was: 'Sufism is singling out the truth from the worn-out trappings of creation.'

Another was Abu Sulyman al-Darani, who died in AD 830, and who said: 'Sufism is the experience of happenings not known except by truth: it is being constantly with this truth in a way known only to God.'

There are hundreds of such definitions concerning this spiritual Way, which have come to fill innumerable pages and which indicate innumerable schools of thought. Most of these, if not all of them, revolve round the relationship between the Creator and the created in worship and personal struggle. All are in accordance with the meaning and the philosophical aims of Sufism. But Sufism itself has evolved and developed, particularly after the philosophical diffusion in the Abbasid period. The thinkers and men of knowledge of that time associated the deeds and sayings of the Sufis with the higher wisdom and the supernatural and the mystical realizations of truth which lay beyond men's ordinary understanding.

The follower of Islamic philosophical history will find that these ideas merged with Sufism as they did with other new and related subjects. So Rabia's Sufism came about after her stringent asceticism coupled with her religious devotion. At the beginning, she was like any other ascetic, praying to God from fear of his punishment and in expectation of his reward. That is the goal of the ascetic. But when she became a Sufi and went deeper into the meaning of worship, she became purified from the sorrows of life and freed from fear of the awesome Day of Judgment. This sincerity in worship, together with her long hours of contemplative thinking about the essence of God and the secrets of the universe, all this caused her soul to break loose and go beyond the unseen world in search of God. At the same time this deep contemplativeness had taken her attention from the affairs of this world. The Sufistic symbolism of her speech imparted what she wished to express, not through the outwardness of language, but through the inner meaning which was far beyond the normal expressive capacity for communicating ideas.

And so it was that Rabia came to be among the earliest of those called Sufis. She was considered one of the Saints whose vision had been raised to see truth. Truth itself has stages, the highest of which is the capacity for pure vision and blessedness.

Her history was not meant to be studied as an academic, scientific exercise; nor to be measured by any psychological yardstick. It shows clearly, even from the few and confused pages of documentation which we have at our disposal, that she did progress from asceticism to Sufism: a natural process in all such sincere, highly gifted people. Rabia was instinctively inclined towards this new Sufi Way, without consciously recognizing its scientific basis, or comprehending the manner in which spiritual awareness evolves. It is likely that she became a Sufi after spending time in the Circles of Recitation which were held in Basra, in order to exercise, praise and rejoice in the love of God with a group of the devout and the seekers. They used to recite the Koran, say the prayers, and chant in special Sufi tones which transmitted a feeling of love and nearness to God. It is also likely that Rabia, in her first encounters with Sufi Circles at an early age, participated in playing the *nay*, a type of reed pipe or flute. This kind of music was an integral part of ancient Sufi movements which are still in existence today. They were like the Assemblies of initiated circles of dervishes that we know in Damascus. In Egypt, too, and other Islamic countries, there are Assemblies of Recitation for both men and women, which take place during the religious processions on festivals and holidays. These still practise the chanting, the playing of the *nay*, the tambourine, and rhythmic drumming. Only in real Sufi Circles, however, is music carefully 'applied'. Elsewhere, everyone takes part or is allowed to hear.

Rabia's Sufism developed as the result of her inborn capacity and vigour, not only from being taught, or from imitating. The seeds were sown in her without her knowing it. The social and religious life in her town was the essential influence. From early childhood, as we have seen, she displayed characteristics similar to those observed in the great ones. She was drawn to the stream of knowledge that so well slaked the thirst in her soul. She found the Higher Love, and was comforted by it. She was like a wanderer in the desert who keeps searching for water until, through exhaustion, he begins to see reflections on the far horizon: an oasis, palm trees with flowing leaves, cool shadows, and streams of nectar. And all these reflections are a mirage. But the traveller never ceases walking towards that vision until he dies of thirst – still short of reaching it. It may well happen that some of those who have been burnt by the blazing sun and lost in these regions have stumbled across an actual oasis, somewhere between life and death. The Sufi must 'die before he dies'.

So it was with Rabia, burnt by the blaze of love in her search for the essence of God. Detaching herself from the created world in all its forms, she was now apart from her ascetic friends who were still desirous. Working towards knowing God alone, searching for a glimpse of his generous face, not wanting payment, not fearing punishment: this was the point at which she parted company from her fear-ridden brethren. Few others, even today, have reached that stage. She moved in search of her own lost self which had far preceded her. With extended wings in a higher, timeless world, her Self appeared, signalling her to follow.

I do not doubt that some great spiritual power had carried Rabia towards this love. When, after long years of dedication, she became engulfed in its incandescent light, she was dazzled by what it revealed. She was not only looking out of herself, but looking into her inner self as well. The Koran had called for deep contemplation of the self and the world within it: 'Do you not look into your own selves?', a magnificent injunction coinciding with Socrates': 'Man, know thyself.' Rabia knew herself well. And so she came to know also the secret world which cannot be seen by eyes, but only by those on whom God has bestowed the capacity of pure vision.

Rabia's prayers were still full of longing, trepidation and entreaty. How often she used to cry out: 'My Lord, if I am worshipping you from fear of fire, burn me in the fires of hell; and if I am worshipping you from desire for paradise, deny me paradise. But if I am worshipping you for yourself alone, then do not deny me the sight of your magnanimous face.'

This prayer is still coming from a lost heart, still questioning and anxious. God has never arranged for his worshippers, or those who do not worship, to know of his intentions. He in his

54

eternal wisdom has knowledge of everything. Rabia as a human being was still a weak creature, longing for comfort, satisfaction of mind, and peace. I do not say this in mitigation: she is far above the need for that. But this idea of worship for worshipping's sake is not dissimilar from today's expression, 'Art for Art's sake', a hypothesis which has been quite roundly refuted. How can art exist only f r itself, when it has so many personal as well as social connotations?

Therefore I say the same about Sufism: worshipping God is for the good of all beings. Serenity, and thankfulness to God, are a great comfort to those who have gone wrong.

The personal psychological consequences of asceticism – the self-centred attitude, the crying, and so on – have a destructiveness in themselves; and also affect the way God planned the actions of the universe to unfold.

In the activity of authentic Sufism, however, experience and the exchange of experiences are the practical and constructive aims. This is very far from the reclusive or intellectual 'Sufism' which is based on superstition, mysteriousness and sentimentality. The world is so full of the latter that this is all that most people 'know' of Sufism.

Even if Rabia in her early asceticism was worshipping for worshipping's sake, we do not blame her as we blame many others from such creeds, young and old, who, having left the world and what was in it, soon became idle. They did no work; they were content to remain reclusive worshippers in the 'Zawias' and in their Mihrabs – in monasteries and at prayer-niches – reciting and praying. They totally missed the point that Islam favoured the active, the industrious man far above the idle one, who consequently missed the delights offered in life and wrongly believed that total abstinence and monasticism, not sincerity and the right approach, led to the gates of heaven.

To reproach the idle man – however sincere in his worship he may be – is more fitting than to reproach an idle woman engrossed in her devotions. Because life, although it requires both sexes to work and sustain themselves, has always expected more from the man, who is not faced with the possibility of early death, as women were especially in Rabia's time. In any case, a woman's devotion to the ideal of motherhood and the home, her struggles and her patience, were widely considered to be far better than any kind of worship . . .

The intention behind Rabia's worship, before she became a Sufi, is evident from what has been written about her disregard for life. This attitude may not have been followed by her for the sake of the Day of Requital. Her answer to a question about heaven makes this plain:

'The neighbour comes before the dwelling.'

The fact that she wanted God only, is evident from a prayer in which she made the plea:

'My Lord, all the good that you have bestowed as my share in this life, give it to your enemies; all that you may have for me in heaven, give it to your Saints. I do not strive except for you alone.'

She was once visited by a man of knowledge from Basra, who started talking about the wretchedness of the world. She gave a deep sigh and said:

'You are a man who must love this world, for he who greatly loves something, keeps talking about it. He who wants to buy new clothes talks about that often. If you had totally freed yourself from this world, it would not have mattered to you: neither its wretchedness nor its goodness.'

In the same way she reprimanded her friends and spiritual brethren, Sufian al-Thawri, Malik Ibn Dinar and Salih Ibn Abd al-Jalil, when in her presence they talked about the evils of the world:

'You have observed the closest thing that lay within your hearts; and so you talk about it.'

Then she turned to Sufian al-Thawri, who was studying under her, and said:

'How excellent a Sufi you might have been, if it were not for your desiring this world.'

He asked:

'Where do you see this desire in me?'

She answered:

'In your speech.'

She was referring to Sufian's long dissertation about the world and its uselessness: a subject much aired among the common people.

Rabia at this stage in her philosophy and her Sufism had become what is described by men of knowledge as the

Visionary, the Glowing One. But this stage in itself was not fulfilling to her. The worry and the wandering of her thoughts were still constantly with her; and this in turn increased her thirst for what lies beyond the existent. She long contemplated the names of God and his attributes, longing to become annihilated in them. She confirmed the songs of unity in her inner consciousness and in her deepest convictions; and this is something which shines only in the hearts of the pure, something which God has given to only a few.

When Rabia had reached the stage of being a Sufi (Sufism has been termed by contemporary Arabs and Orientalists 'theosophy', the mystical insight into knowledge), only then did she experience peace, and breathe the tranquil perfume of eternity. She stood on the shores of infinity, transparent in her purity of soul. She had experienced a shift from existence in the world to existence in an inward isthmus. There she found God, through an absolute emptiness impossible to describe. How very lengthy the arguments have been: about the stages of Sufi development, and the Islamic philosophical enquiry into the 'Sifatyyn' and the creed of Mutazila, 'The Separatists'. And after all the analysis carried out by the philosophers and the men of knowledge, with all their inventiveness, unnecessary quarrelling and tedious argument, they arrived at the realization that the true essence of a thing cannot be described by material examples. Yet Rabia had understood all that simply through her heart, her scrupulous consciousness and her penetrating insight. The wings which had carried her to the heights of contemplation, brought her to rest among gardens where birds on the branches sang tenderly in a breeze flowing towards a state of being that knows no twilight, and an abundance that has no end.

VII

THE LOVING OF GOD

Women like Majnun's Layla or Romeo's Juliet, who were the victims of love and longing, had become intoxicated with human adoration, and inflamed with desire: all seemingly in vain. Their stories were marvellous examples of forbearance, pain and self-annihilation for the sake of the beloved mortal they were prohibited from seeing. Their hopes were shattered. But they did not look up to heaven with tear-filled eyes to ask anything of God except that he ease the pain of love. There are an incalculable number of such individuals in the history of love: they portray the passions and the modesty, the chaste, the yearning and the playful ones. All have idolised the mortal man, and found the world and this rapture to be the very blessing of this life.

But Rabia's love was of a finer order. She could disdain the human, she was impelled towards the highest ideals; she even went beyond that, to become consumed in a sublime love not experienced before by any formalist Muslim.

Only when she had been submerged in Sufism and wisdom, and had acquired unerring inner vision, only then was she lifted up to seek the face of God alone. Only then could she knock and ask at the higher door. As I can imagine the story of the Miraj, the journey of the Prophet Muhammed to Paradise, and the ascent of the perfected human soul towards the eternal, so I can imagine Rabia in her search for the essence of God, passing beyond the comprehensible until she touched a kind of love purified of sorrow and guilt. She became as light as the soul attached to her body, floating in her worship higher and higher, as does a balloon: the lighter it grows, the higher it goes into the heavens.

However great the linear advances in contemporary psychology – that new study unknown to our predecessors – it will never explain the science of the self or the doctrines of the soul. Its biggest perplexity lies in research about love and attraction; it is always assuming, imagining, guessing and failing accurately to analyse; very rarely succeeding. As human faces differ from one another, so do the potentialities of different individuals: mood, vibration and love. It is love's habit to be born without the lovers' consent. Whoever resists it, falls the sooner wounded by it. The eyes are the means to the heart, except for the blind lover, whose hearing is the way.

Until the hour of her death, she loved her Master the Creator; not the master who had bought, owned and then freed her: not the one who had disappointed her and broken her heart. After her deep immersion in Sufism, and her constant sacrament of worship, something was born in her soul. It was love: but not ordinary love. Her beloved was not seen; but he was reflected in all the perfection of his attributes and in all the universes and in every one of his signs. The oneness of the cosmos showed her God and his love in every particle. The road was wide open to her.

Here is a glimpse into Rabia's expression of this love which had tamed her, sensitized her consciousness, and filled her power of belief to overflowing. She spoke to her only Beloved with humility and reverence:

'My Lord, never have I listened to any creature's voice, nor the whisper of the trees, nor the purling of water, nor birdsong, nor the flickering of shadow, nor the roaring of the wind, nor the crash and rattle of thunder, without finding it a witness to your oneness, and evidence that there is nothing like unto you.'

Another example, alight with the burning desire of a heart solely occupied by the wish to be lost in God, is shown in this interchange. She had been asked:

'Do you love Satan, O Rabia, or do you hate him?'

She replied:

'The amount of love I have for my Lord fully protects me from the activity of hating Satan.'

Her questioners sought to compel her, and asked further:

'Do you love the Prophet, peace be upon him?'

And Rabia replied:

'By God, I love him indeed. But the love I have for the Creator has fully occupied me and prevented me from loving the created.'

59

These words were never intended to show disrespect for the Prophet . . .

Her point was that there was not space left in her heart for wholly and truly loving anything but God. We find al-Manawi in his book *The Ranks of the Saints*, saying:

'Rabia in her prayers used to prostrate herself a thousand times during the day and night; and when she was asked, "What do you seek from all this?" she answered: "I do not seek recompense. I do this so that the Prophet of God may be pleased, and may say to the other Prophets: 'Look, there is a woman of my people; and this is her work.' " '

Rabia, therefore, did want to please the Prophet, peace be upon him: she wished for all women to be honoured by her example. She loved him and wished to meet him on the Day of Requital.

Each time she whispered to her Lord in her prayers, she made her plea and assured him:

'Esteemed Lord, it is not for your heaven but for your love that I have spent my life worshipping you.

'Oh God, will you burn the heart that loves you, and a tongue that never ceases from praising you, and a slave that fears you?'

It appears to non-Sufi commentators that this long-buried fear of the fires of hell returned to her in spite of the new attitude of liberation in her worship: 'Neither from fear of hell, nor for reward in heaven.' None can escape from what he sees or hears. A certain sight takes the memory back to all that has been associated with it; and when Rabia happened to see fire, her heart jumped in her breast. The fear would not last for long, it was said; but she would cry, as if to put out the flames, each time she saw fire. And when she looked at water, she would feel a coolness within, and a mellow sense of well-being. These two eternal elements, fire and water, haunted her – in a sense that was beyond magic or alchemy. They seemed to intertwine in her mind during the soft music and chanting of the religious ceremonies, manifesting to her as a symbol that both healed the darkness and gave light to broken hearts in need of hope. One day she was seen running quickly, carrying a bucket of water with one hand and a firebrand with the other. On being asked, 'Where are you going, Rabia?' she answered:

'To throw the fire to heaven, and to pour the water on hell; so that these can no longer be a cause of worshipping God: nor will his creatures look to the Lord for material incentive or for spiritual reward.'

Thus she taught her contemporaries by object-lessons; and was often misunderstood. This demonstration symbolized the idea of reward and punishment which she sought to abolish, because they had both good and evil within them. She looked for a free kind of worship untainted by expectation of thanks or recompense. From the religious point of view this idea cannot be realized on this Earth. It seems too idealistic and theoretical: more than can be expected from human beings. But Rabia sought to be free: free from worshipping even God himself, if it were done from a sense of servitude. She wished to worship as a totally liberated human being with a choice of her own.

She had visualized this spiritual love in her Sufism, and she sincerely and wholly believed in it. Like a houri who has become a Saint through her prayers and altered aims, Rabia developed this ultimate veracity. She carried a stick, but was herself a living branch; she wore an old patched mantle, and put on worn-out sandals with her toes exposed. People considered her an aimless wanderer.

But Rabia came to be her own companion; and she knew the truth behind the manifest. Yet she remained thirsty for the ultimate secret of creation. She allayed these longings through contemplation. Beautiful scenes appeared to her and she heard herself being called, as has been reported of Joan of Arc who went to the flames. Rabia herself had escaped fire and wanted no one to experience its torture. Its flames were always burning in her mind, and she did not want her love-filled heart to be scorched and melted. She had already been tamed by the flame of love. If she could come to our Earth today, she would find that certain ideas which she had attempted to communicate spiritually had been translated scientifically into knowledge and inventions which have changed the face of the world altogether. The secret of atomic power, which baffled the Greeks for so long, has been solved. It has opened the door to knowledge in a way which would show Rabia to be of great value: not so much in terms of mathematics or electricity, but in her cognition of God and the spiritual, which in her own case was able, as it were, to bombard the atom in Rabia's own Self. Once this atom has been exploded in man the purer essence is released, as Shabistari has it, in *The Secret Garden*.

Rabia's love was not like the love known to the Greeks, which came from the teachings of Plato; nor like the pre-Islamic love familiar to the monks. Her uniquely woven model entered the Islamic creeds as a concept of beauty dissociated from the body. How often I remember the story of Orpheus playing his lyre music in the Regions of Hell: capturing the attention of those unfortunates being tortured so that they no longer felt the pain. I see Rabia's faint image on the shimmering waves: not in worn-out dress and sandals, with a stick; but moving towards the shores of heaven in a halo of brightness, with a reed pipe, playing the tune for her verses:

'I love you with two kinds of love:
A fervent love, and a love you are worthy of.
Of the fervent love: I am too consumed in commemorating
    you to remember anyone but you.
And of the love that you are worthy of: it is for unveiling
    yourself for me to see.
So there is nothing to thank me for in either love: the
    thanks are to you in both.'

Several Sufis have explained the meaning behind these famous verses, as have others studying Sufism from the outside. They have interpreted it according to Rabia's spiritual propensity, and also to what agrees with the accepted nature of Sufi understanding. So their conclusions about this twin love, or the two kinds of love referred to by Rabia, are apposite. They have delved deep into the object and the range of this spiritual force that ought not to resemble the human affections. And they have interpreted the first kind as a Sufi love that transcends mere worship. This then becomes transmuted into an aspect of God. Abu Talib al-Makki, in his book *The Sustenance of Hearts*, wrote:

'The fervent and the worthy love both need explanation, until it becomes clear to him who does not know. It must also be experienced by him who has not seen it. Therefore intellectual labelling and descriptions, even when used by an intelligent man, are an hypocrisy if he lacks the capacity and taste to savour the difference between the two loves. But in summing-up, we can only point it out to the one who knows. The first verse means: "I saw you and came to you from the certitude of seeing; not from a belief formed from propaganda and hearsay, or from reasons of ambition or emotion, which could easily cause my love to change according to changes of circumstance. Rather, my love is from the path of seeing. So I came close to you, I fled the world for you, and I have been occupied completely with you since first I devoted myself to you." '

As for the second kind of love, al-Makki's interpretation is:

'This is the sublime love for the majesty of God. It comes not from ambition nor from any sensory joy. Nor does it deserve any reward for that.'

Almost unanimously, the interpreters of these two kinds of love have agreed that the real fervent love is for God alone. They also agree about the second kind: that God is most worthy of it. He allowed Rabia to see his face in the first and also the second instance: thanks be to him for that privilege. Abu Hamid al-Ghazzali, in his book *The Revival of Religious Sciences*, associated himself with this interpretation when he wrote:

'Rabia in her "fervent" love meant only God's love, and his generous benefactions. Loving God "for his worthiness" meant to love him for his beauty and splendour which he made clear for her to see. And that is the higher of the two loves.'

The higher of the two loves, the more precious in al-Ghazzali's eyes and in the eyes of others, produces a conscious longing for the face of God, and gratitude for his mercy. It totally preoccupies one from remembering the world. Rabia on the whole did not find herself worthy of this love: on the contrary, she thought that however hard she tried, she might not be recompensed on the Final Day. She was often frightened that she had not done enough; so she annihilated herself in worship. He alone was her guide and her means to

63

the Higher Love. From him came the inspiration uttered by her on the meaning of that Higher Love which was free of all fetters.

All the interpreters who have held similar opinions on Rabia's spiritual love have missed the saying of one great poet who must have observed in his own time, or at the time of Rabia, the various approaches of numerous spiritual creeds. I am speaking of Abu Nawas, who surpasses all others in his portrayal of the unique sensation he experiences when drinking:

'I get two blows
While the boon companion gets but one:
This is a distinction bestowed on me
And the privilege is only mine.'

These 'double-strength' feelings, in love or in other matters, are contained in the theory of subjects studied by contemporary philosophers and psychologists. If the spiritual capacity in a man is unleashed, it resembles the igniting of gunpowder. All the heroism and the genius in history have been the result of such explosions of capacity. Holy men who have worshipped God and lived their Sufism in true sincerity have all undergone the experience of their undammed human consciousness being doubled or multiplied. Rabia in her twin love found blessedness of heart; she also found a blessing in the pain that came with it. She experienced a kind of spiritual release during her sufferings. But her single-mindedness of thought and contemplation could also distract her from physical feeling.

On one occasion, while she was in prayer on her reed mat, a small fragment of reed got into her eye; and she continued the prayer, impervious to the pain. Another time, standing up in full view of a number of other people, she hit her head against a wall. It was a fearful wound, but she did not show any signs of pain. The people around her came running to comfort her, and were amazed at her stoicism.

She said:

'I am too occupied obeying his will. As to what happened just now, I did not feel what you saw.'

It appears from these words that her deep concentration and contemplation allowed her to become aware of nothing but the object of her thought. This is borne out by what has been said by Farid al-Din al-Attar, in his book, *The Recital of the Saints*:

'Her friends came to see her and learn from her, and they discussed and enquired into many things. On one occasion they talked about Sufism and worship. Another day, when Sufian al-Thawri and al-Balkhi and Malik Ibn Dinar were present, along with other ascetics, Rabia asked them what was meant by truthfulness. One of them answered: "He is not truthful in his claims who has not endured God's punishment." Rabia said, "That is pride."

'A second person, wishing to give an opinion which would win her admiration, said: "He is not truthful in his claims who has not thanked God for his punishment." Rabia said nothing, and showed no reaction. Turning to Malik Ibn Dinar, as if testing his understanding of the subtleties of expression, the other said:

' "He is not truthful in his claims who has not enjoyed God's punishment."

'Then Rabia smiled, and said with a kind of joy: "But there is, O Malik, a better thing than all of you have said . . ." So they immediately asked her, "You say it then, and give us your opinion." She replied: "He is not truthful in his claims who has not forgotten the punishment while seeing his Lord." They all fell silent, submitting to her unsurpassed vision.'

There was something in her words reminiscent of the story of the Egyptian women who absent-mindedly cut and wounded their hands while lost in admiration of the handsome Yusuf, when he had been ordered by al-Aziz's wife to enter in upon them. Looking at him, they all gave praise to God, and asked forgiveness from al-Aziz's wife for their having scorned her deep passion for Yusuf. They forgot their wounds in their enthralment at the sight of his beauty.

Rabia, to increase the adeptness of her companions, had asked them about truthfulness. Now she asked them how generosity was counted among them.

Sufian al-Thawri replied: 'For the people of the world, it is generosity with their money; but among the people of the coming world, it is generosity with themselves.'

Rabia said: 'You menfolk are all wrong!'

Sufian asked: 'What is generosity among womenfolk?'

Rabia answered: 'It is worshipping him out of love for him: not in expectation of a recompense or reward.'

It seems from that and other conversations which are related of Rabia and her Sufi and ascetic friends, that she always had the final say. They all confessed their gratitude to her, and to her profoundness of speech. They counted her their mentor, their teacher, and adviser on every subject.

Salih al-Marri the Sufi used to attend her Assembly and listen to her, to increase his knowledge and clarify in his mind certain things he had missed. When she heard him say more than once:

'When someone keeps knocking at the door, it will in time open for him!' Rabia replied, reprimanding him: 'How long will you keep saying that? When was the door ever closed, that it might have to open?'

Salih understood, and said: 'An ignorant old man; and a woman who knows.'

Thus this great Sufi Salih verified Rabia's knowledge and wisdom, as did many of his disciples after him. As for the idea of the unity of God, she appeared boundless in her observation. Her concept of the essence of God transcended chains and limits, for she well knew that God's door is without hinge or key. This door was, at the same time, a symbol of a vast system, unbounded, unattainable, engulfing the earth and all the universes.

Those words of the venerable Salih are reminiscent of a similar interchange, when a major Caliph, the just Umar Ibn al-Khattab, publicly recognized the wisdom of a woman and pronounced her the correct and perceptive one. He was addressing the people on an issue concerning women's rights and their inheritance, when he mentioned that 'the most abhorred form of legitimacy to God is divorce.' A woman standing by, listening to him, contradicted him and pointed out his fault. And he said to her: 'Here is a mistaken man and a correct woman.'

Rabia was venerated and found most worthy by knowledgeable men, when they realized she was as one of them; and furthermore that she surpassed them in her Sufism. No man ever showed reverence for any woman except after clear assurance of her merit. Such is the nature of man, anywhere, any time. Rabia no doubt felt secure in her position, so became creative in her form of expression. No symbol or explanation was too difficult for her.

One man of knowledge said to her: 'You are magnificent in your speech: would you not qualify as a garrison?' Rabia answered: '*I am*, indeed, a garrison; for I do not let anything within me escape, nor do I let anything external penetrate.'

Her questioner had wanted to test her excellence by comparing her with the men of the garrison of the land who stood vigil within their forts to defend the people against the enemy, and who were known to be heroic men of superior power and dangerous attributes. Rabia was amused by the analogy, and in saying that she herself was a garrison, she was likening every man's life to a breach which the enemy is about to enter, the moment a sleeping guard gives him the chance. The enemy is the evil deed in humanity, and man ought to stand constantly on guard from within the walls of his inner self, to protect it from the hidden infiltrator.

So we see how Rabia excelled in her symbolic and overt illustrations. In her conversations and everyday speech, she makes analogies and equivocations, and wanders about in her symbolism. But, when portraying the higher love of God, her words become unveiled from ambiguity. She utters straightforward rhymes and verses full of Sufic meaning; as we find in her answer to a question as to how she arrived at this love:

'There is no in-between in a lover and his beloved. It is an utterance born from longing, a description from tasting. He who tastes, knows. He who describes, distorts. And how do you describe something in whose presence you are no more; and in whose being you persevere, and with whose evidence you go on?

'Reverence makes the tongue dumb. Bewilderment prevents the coward from declaration, jealousy veils the eyes from alteration, and amazement binds the mind from testifying; so that there is nothing but continual astonishment and perplexity, with hearts wandering and secrets hidden.'

It is not surprising that such a portrayal should have come from Rabia, the unconsidered slave who had mastered the art of eloquence. It seems that the oppressed slave, an uneducated slum-dweller, had become a woman of transparent honesty and gentility who found the need for a subtle command of language to express what she had felt and suffered. A new self must have emerged in the process. We are not, however, certain that everything attributed to Rabia was in fact hers: the spread of this kind of speech had not started during the early Islamic era, but much later, with the arrival of the skilled literary Sufi teachers. All those rhymed words were as if magnetised with energy from the heart; in deep, sincere and pure remembrance of God. But some could easily have been said by another person. If doubt exists about some of the sayings of the Prophet himself, we ought to be cautious about all that is said to have come to us from Rabia, this early Sufi and Lover of God, bearing in mind the effect which the various other spiritual creeds had on early Islam.

But Rabia's soul was flowing through the words quoted above, as if she wanted to return to them, and live with them. She reached a degree of transcendence so high that it became evident from her Assemblies, especially towards the end of her life, that she wanted to obliterate all obstacles, when she said: 'Between myself and God there is no in-between.'

This is a dangerous and most daring claim: to drop the distance between God the Creator and the created. The difference is essential between the two; and Rabia's state of spiritual exaltation does not, in my opinion, justify her speaking as she did, however sincerely. The dignity of worship remains a noble ideal.

We do not know the ways of the spiritually adept; but it seems as if Rabia began, in some of her recitations and spiritual activities, to behave like a child who contradicts its parents' instructions. The Sufi literature does not, however, prohibit that: nor is it rejected by the Seekers and Enthralled Ones. An example of what has been attributed to Rabia in this vein is her saying:

'My cup, my wine and the Companion are three, and I, filled with yearning love, make four.
The lasting cup of joy and happiness is handed by the cupbearer to each one in succession.
If I look, I look only for him, and if I arrive I cannot see without him.

68

Do not blame me: I love his beauty, and, by God, my ears
    cannot hear your reproval.
How often, from ardour and bitter attachment, have I
    caused streams to flow from my tearful eyes.
Neither my teardrops cease, nor my being with him lasts,
    Nor will my sore eyes sleep.'

These seductive verses have a most beautiful artistic
expression; and although my portrayal of them may show
some loss in quality, it has not been done without care and
love.

Amorous poetry, however ardent, has limits which should
not be exceeded, and these limits are what will determine the
reader's sympathy. The sanctity of worship should be kept
holy; and I believe that this informality on Rabia's part is not
compatible with the nature of supplication. To call on God in
the name of this love, like one mortal talking to another, has
caused some criticism and opposition.

It is not surprising that, when Rabia spoke in verse, her
heart poured poetry onto her tongue: the language of her
time was so expressive. There is no doubt that her religious
studies had helped her in her citing of the Traditions, prayers
and proverbs. Her splendid Sufic symbolology and precision
of language was followed by the later Sufi poets, who
diversified this art in even newer ways beyond formerly
known limits. They used concealed meanings and hidden
analogies. This was their holy wine, their nearness to God,
and their spiritual intoxicant. This kind of Sufi hymn
resembled the traditional religious chants and commemora-
tions.

Rabia's poetry and Sufi sayings were of this character:
either a call of longing, wavering sentiment and dreams; or a
rhyming hymn to be chanted in the Sufi circle and in the
assemblies of the pious. Although none can confirm exactly
which were spoken by Rabia, these are examples said to have
been composed by her to invoke a blessing, or as a supplication to God:

'Oh, my joy, my wish, my support,
My friend, my esteemed one and my intention,
You are the soul of my heart; you are my hope.

69

You are my comfort, and your desire is my food.
How very many blessings you have given me, and pleasures
    and capacities.
Now your love is my desire and my heaven:
It is a clearance to my captured heart's eye.
As long as I may live I will not be apart from you.
You are my strength when I am in darker mood.
If you are pleased with me, then, oh my heart's desire,
My happiness has begun.'

When she was asked about her solitude and contentment,
and how she had left her friends, she said:

'My comfort, O my brethren, is in my solitude,
And my Beloved is always within my own presence.
I have found no substitute for his love;
And his love in the desert sands is my harrow.
If I die of longing and he is still not satiated,
How great my pain – how great my eternal sorrow.
Forsaking all creation, aspiring to your love-token, this
    truly is the quest I follow.'

The composition of this poetry, as I have said, in its
balance, utterance and meaning, indicates the nature of the
chanting practised in the Sufi commemorative circles. It also
accords with Rabia's other poetic words inspired by her
observance of the vigilant Sufi religious nights. She had
broken through a poetic barrier unheard of before, with her
'Longing Poetry.' Several contemporary investigators have
long studied this subject. The orientalists, the Western
students of the East, have been most unfair to Rabia. None
has done any special psychological research or organized
study to unveil the obscure in her life and bring to light the
truth. They have often described her higher love as an
ordinary love of passion, because they have not found anyone
earlier who loved as Rabia did. They became suspicious of
her Islamic background and Sufistic teachings.
    In Christianity, love is the religion. Christ, peace be upon
him, wandered preaching this love, and the history of
Christianity is full of the lives of Saints, men and women who
kneeled praying in the churches or monasteries, separated
and cut off from the world. And if their soft footsteps could

talk, moving like a gentle breeze on the flagstones of the nunnery, while their figures expressed complete absorption, their bright crosses dangling from their necks, they would have testified that 'We have seen the Higher Love.' They would not be speaking of the love of people for people. And the researchers did not consider it a love of passion, but called it the ideal love: that which was preached by Christ, peace be upon him. The term 'ardent love' is not mentioned in the Koran, nor in the traditions of the Prophet, because it means something beyond love. So it will not have significance except for the one who has stepped beyond the normally understood meaning of the word. Islamic Sufism, in its early conception and life, resembles a city surrounded by a high wall, with guards posted on top: none may enter without permission. It has its own special language and specific symbolology; and a secret word that breaks any chain and unlocks any lock. The true Sufi language has its dictionary in the minds and in the expressions of its people. Though the real meanings of this symbolology have not been published, the Sufis nevertheless have preserved a diction and a dictum of the symbols. If we give due honour to all the contributors in this language, we find that Rabia established publicly many of the first words in this dictionary. She was also the first to explain the Higher Love in Islamic Sufism. When that particular love word appeared at the gates of that walled city, the guardians, themselves Sufi veterans of this word, were reluctant that it should penetrate their vocabulary and assemblies, claiming that it was from Judaeo-Christian material, or from the Platonic tradition; and that the normally used word 'love' was more proper. But considering the source and the barrier of the word, and to please the originator of their city, the gates were opened to Rabia, their distinguished guest.

And thus the word *Ishq* – divine love – entered, merging into the Sufi dictionary. It took the history of an unique Muslim woman, forerunner even to the men, to explain how these three Arabic letters (*ayn*, *shin*, *qaf*) give meaning to the word: Its penetrating eye (*ayn*), its burning desire (*shin*), and its big heart (*qaf*).* Rabia's faith is almost beyond the sphere

---

* The word *Ishq* (love) is conceived here as comprising the capital letters of three Arabic words: *Ayn* (eye); *Shawq* (desire) and *Qalb* (heart).

of religion. If we could count all the worshippers of God from the beginning, we should find thousands upon thousands waiting for their turn to enter heaven. And if Ridwan stood at its gate, not permitting anyone to enter except those who had in this world loved the face of God alone, they would all be turned away, except a small company with Rabia at their head. For Rabia is the one who originated the idea of purity in religion, and the absence of any hope of gain from it. As I write, I am thinking of a poem by that poet of the Lebanon, Gibran, portraying the covetousness behind worship:

> 'Religion is a field unplanted except by those who accomplish an interest from it – return.
> If it were not from fear of hell, none would worship any god;
> And if not for the expected rewards, they would deny God.'

Rabia has the honour to be one of the first to express this Higher Love in sincerity and truthfulness. She was a remarkable Sufi teacher, and a prime example of piety, belief and knowledge of certainty: like her predecessors Dhun-Nun the Egyptian, and Ibn al-Farid and Ibn al-Arabi, and the others who followed the Sufi Way and reached the saintly ranks.

VIII

FROM SLAVE TO HOLY WOMAN

For every beginning there is an outcome; for every cause – whether of force, energy, attribute or talent – there is an effect. If we were to ask every distinguished, every industrious person, 'What was it that first motivated or attracted you?' they would say: 'The starting-point was pain, love, hunger or revenge.' There are many reasons for this surge of energy: for the first assault and the determining shock. In Rabia's case, she had in her early life tasted fear and hunger, deprivation and disgrace. The turning-point was her release, her emancipation. It was also her reason for turning her face towards the higher aim and the distant dream. And because she has not written her own biography, nor left for the ages to come very much evidence to make her familiar to us, Rabia needs some of her hidden story to be brought to life. The lack of evidence has caused many a sincere writer to accept the word of those researchers and historians who have fabricated tales about her, and attributed sayings to her of which she was innocent. Each of us has but a small candle of light; and we are unable to move through all her scattered treasures. Some things are hidden; others have been dispersed over the years.

The route that Rabia travelled with such dedication and faith was bedevilled by fierce feelings: first, the desperation to be rid of her bondage, which burned in her and stole her youth. Second, she was never really free from the stigma, however much the situation after her release may have changed for the better.

Historical documents show that Rabia was from the Mawali family of al-Atik, who were connected to Banu Adwa, and whose surname she assumed, in accordance with established custom. Al-Atik were from the tribe of Qais; and so Rabia was named al-Qaisiya.

There has been much confusion, and differing opinions, regarding the kindred of this Sufi lover. Writers have been

73

unable to distinguish between Rabia's sayings and the sayings of other Sufi women named after her, who also lived a hard ascetic life, and produced sayings and poetry on worship and spiritual love.

Rabia had an unquenchable desire for freedom, in quest of which so many before and since have undergone hardship and calamities. Each time they succeeded in undoing one link in the chain of bondage, they longed to destroy another and then another, until every link should be undone. But they could not always destroy them all; and therein lay grief and regret. Rabia, suffering and being antagonized by slavery, concentrated on one anxiety, to obtain full freedom and be rid of all the links to her oppression by man. She grew bewildered and fearful, she lost her youth; she was sold like a chattel and disappointed by men. She wandered in the desert lands with a restless passion, until she became truly liberated.

All this created a great surge of energy within her, impelling her onward like a storm-wind crossing the skies, cleansed from the decadence of the world and the burden of men. She felt elevated like a pure breeze. And so all her effort after being freed was directed to entering the ranks of the ascetics, the Sufis and the dedicated ones. Having tasted liberty, and felt it deep within body and soul, having broken from the human oppressor, she consecrated herself to God and his worship. He was to be her one and only Lord. She could no longer bear servitude to man in any form whatever.

So Rabia became sanctified through religion and faith. She had a pure spirit, praying hands, and received answers to her pleas. She became known among the people as the Trust-worthy and the Destitute. They came to ask for her blessing and love, offering whatever God had offered them. And she always refused to accept anything, returning their gifts with thanks.

One day when Sufian al-Thawri came to see Rabia, he found a merchant standing at her door, glum-faced. He asked him what he wanted. The man answered: 'I have brought a sack full of gold coins, dinars, to offer as a gift to Rabia, to help her subsistence. But I fear she will refuse to take it. Can you persuade her to accept it?' So they both entered, and the merchant gave Rabia the money. She immediately started crying, and looking up towards the heavens, said: 'He knows that I am ashamed to ask for the things of this world from its owner: how can I accept this now, from someone who does not own it?'

Another merchant arrived with a thousand silver dirhams, and offered Rabia a house. It seems that this time she gave in to his insistence, and went to the house. No sooner had she got there than she fell deep into contemplation of the decorating and colours, as if she were a totally different woman. But she soon started up, begging forgiveness for the lapse; and she went to the owner of the house to return his gift, saying: 'I fear that my heart may become attached to your house; and it will distract me from working for the Day of Judgment. All my desire is to be always worshipping God completely and wholly.'

Her friends tried never to let a day pass without seeing her; they were always happy to learn from her and receive her guidance. But she refused help from any one of them.

Malik Ibn Dinar, visiting her one day, found her on an old straw mat spread on the floor, drinking from a broken jug, her armrest made of clay. Broken-hearted, he said: 'Oh, Rabia, I have wealthy friends. If only you would allow me to ask them to give something to you!'

She answered: 'That is not the right thing to say, O Malik. God provides for me, as he provides for them. Does the one who provides for the rich forget to provide for the poor? If that is indeed his way, then we for our part are fully content with it.'

When Sufian al-Thawri, her closest friend, asked her, 'Rabia, what is your heart's need?' (referring, it seems, to food), she replied: 'How do you, O Sufian, ask me that; and you know me the best? God well knows that twelve years ago, and for the first time, I really wanted to eat some dates – and they are abundant in Basra. But I have not eaten them to this very day. I am a slave only to him; and I have not the capacity to behave according to my own heart's desire: because if I want, and God does not want that for me, then that is ingratitude.' So Sufian yielded to her conviction, saying, 'Be that as it may, O Rabia: I cannot talk to you about your business, so talk to me about my business.'

Rabia smiled at him, and said: 'If it were not for your attraction to this world, you would have been an unimpeachable man.' Sufian was ashamed and looked down. Then he raised his eyes, weeping, and said: 'My Lord, I wish you could be pleased with me!'

Rabia retorted:

'Are you not ashamed of yourself, asking God to be pleased with you, when you do nothing to please him?' This and many similar stories about Rabia confirm her total indifference as to whether she had food or not, whether she was tired or not; happy or unhappy, it was all the same to her. Her Sufism had raised her to a state of understanding consciousness which was at the same time most silent and calm; so she could scarcely tell – was it she who lived, or was it another person?

In her state of detachment, she seemed to dissolve within herself; the walls swayed, and she was powerless to intervene – as if she really were someone else and not herself. Her *muridin* (followers) and friends came to glorify her; but she shunned praise and attachment to herself. She debarred them from contaminating her with their emotion. I can imagine her moving through the markets of Basra, or sitting in solitude, feeling sorry for all the people she met, whose bitterness tainted her spiritual world and the true state of her being.

The true holy person or saint never takes advantage of a God-given faculty; and Rabia was never a hypocrite, or an opportunist. She refused all human aid, because it came from someone like herself: a mortal being. Others before her had accepted such inducements, and been manipulated by the donor. God is the only real giver. Yet Rabia not only refused gifts from man: she also refused to ask God for anything. She saw that the affairs of the world are nobody's business, nobody's property: that life is, rather, a naked thing – a passing from hand to hand. Creation is the property of the Creator, and man passes through life to complete a task or convey a message: then he is gone, and others come in his place. So the immortal, the one who has gone, serves the mortal in spite of himself, whether willingly or unwillingly. Therefore was he not to be shunned, the one who extended a hired hand, offering borrowed presents?

Rabia in fact had a brilliantly stable mind; and never conducted herself in many of the ways expected of so-called 'holy' men and women. She never appeared absent-minded, or claimed indulgence for living 'on a higher plane'. It distressed her to see the common misapprehensions about her, and she often avoided people: harshly refused to see them, too, at times.

She was once questioned: 'God has crowned the heads of the Saints with gifts of blessing, and their speech as well. How did you reach such a stage of sainthood?'

She said: 'By both my words and my actions . . . God, I seek your protection from all who divert me from you, and from anyone who becomes an obstacle between you and me!'

When they insisted on knowing the secret of her saintliness, and hinted that she might not after all be such a person, her womanly pride was touched. She replied: 'What you have said may well be true as far as women are concerned, for women have never thought themselves worthy of such a high state of blessedness. But remember, no woman has ever claimed that she was a prophet, or claimed to be holy . . .'

Rabia said this knowing her people and her times very well. It was the era of the Carmathians and of those who claimed prophethood: of people who rebelled against Islam and confiscated the property of Muslims. This iconoclasm was carried close to the Kaaba itself; but none of those who committed these transgressions were other than men. And Rabia did not stop there; she made it clear that the common belief that women were basically unchaste, was a falsehood: that it was in fact the male himself who was the cause of a woman's corruption. This belief still lingers to this very day. Yet man is always responsible for a woman's behaviour in life. In the home and in society, he is her mirror-image and model. So why should any man have regarded it as beyond the capacity of a woman like Rabia to receive the approval of God and be among the blessed ones, knowing that the great ascetics had acquired wisdom and become Adepts through her Sufism and her conduct? It is hard for man to rid himself of inherited compulsions and prejudice – in spite of full evidence that pious and devout women do exist.

Yet it was a woman who became the first ascetic in Islam from whose heart a spring of the knowledge of God was struck. Rabia herself declined to be counted among the blessed, and never regarded these manifestations as miracles, or even dream fulfilments or knowledge of the mysteries, as her Sufi contemporaries and those who came after her thought. That is what was impressive about Rabia's miracles and blessed munificence, which were perhaps coincidences at some times, but were actual happenings at others. The naive comprehend miracles they have heard of; but only as far as these agree with their own superficial interpretations. Or they may believe everything from hearsay, without questioning it.

So with the story mentioned in newspapers some time ago, about the miracle of the coffin of one of the pious men in an Egyptian village, which persistently refused to be carried in any direction other than the one it wanted. This is similar to what sometimes actually happens.

Some historians and researchers into Sufism have actually invented such miracles and attributed them to Rabia, pandering to the superstitions of the ignorant. The Sufi Farid al-Din al Attar was among those who wrote about her the most. He honoured the blessings with which she was endowed, and told strange tales about her. One related how a herd of gazelles kept running away from people, but were at peace in Rabia's presence. When she was asked to explain this, she said: 'The gazelles flee from those who eat their meat.'

In another story, this Sufi who was enchanted by Rabia recounted how one of the ascetics came to her asking for food. She put a pot of meat to cook – without lighting a fire under it. Then she and her companion started talking about the knowledge of God, and forgot about the pot. After the night's prayer, she went and emptied out a stew of fully cooked meat. Another time, according to Attar, a thief entered her house, and found nothing but a jug of water. As he turned to leave, Rabia said to him, 'If you are true to your beliefs, you will not leave without taking something with you.' The thief replied: 'I could find nothing.'

'You poor man,' said Rabia, 'Take this jug and perform the ablutions. Then enter this niche and pray twice – and you will leave with something.'

The thief did as she suggested. Then Rabia looked up to the heavens and said: 'My Lord and Master, this man has come to my door and found nothing from me. So I have made him stand at your door: please do not deny him your favour and your reward.'

When the man had finished, he found comfort, and he

continued praying all night long. At dawn, Rabia found him prostrate, reproaching himself and saying:

'If my Lord asked me: "Are you not ashamed to disobey me?
You hide your sins from the people, and with disobedience you come to me?"
How then shall I answer when he reproaches and enquires of me?'

Rabia asked him: 'Dear friend, how was your night?' And he replied: 'It was good. I stood and commended myself into the hands of my Lord, with all my humiliation and poverty, and he accepted my reasons and healed my dishonoured way. He forgave my sins, and answered my requests . . .' And the man walked out of her place, bewildered. Rabia raised her hands to heaven and said: 'My Lord and my Master, this man has stood at your door one hour and you have accepted him; while I, ever since I have known you, have placed myself in your hands. Have you, I wonder, accepted me?' And, as al-Attar relates, a voice answered Rabia from within, saying: 'Oh Rabia, we have for your sake accepted him; and because of you, have drawn him closer to us.'

These accounts of miraculous happenings, probably invented to show Rabia's elevated state and to confirm her place among the ranks of the Saints and friends of God, were not limited to tales about her life; they included stories about her after death, and dreams illustrating the high status she had attained in her Lord's company. Other dreams relate conversations and admonitions between Rabia and her peers, again as assurances of her high standing on the Day of Requital. But these happenings which have come down to us seem more like myth than reality. We look at them through our scientifically educated eyes; and this, together with psychological interpretation, enables us to study Rabia as she should be studied.

We have all known in our time of Indian mystics who sleep on beds of nails, who have the ability to reduce their heart-rate, or who, after being buried in sand, are recovered still alive. These people roam through East and West, astonishing the observers, mystifying the physicians and reducing scientific interpretation to near helplessness in the face of the apparent magic. Some have interpreted it as a kind of self-

79

hypnosis; or as mass hypnosis of the audience during the performance.

We know of hypnotists today who, concentrating the gaze of their subject, can send him or her to sleep; and then, after asking a number of questions, are said to induce them at a command to rise slowly into the air. The hypnotist may guide the subject a little; but there is no physical support; and then, after a sign or spoken word, he or she is returned to their original state. Some investigators have explained these capacities as spiritual or psychological powers. In every human being there is a magnetic force, strong or weak; and he who has it and can use it, would be able to do such things as I have described.

It is not unlikely that the Sufi Rabia may have possessed such magnetism, through her strong character, her personality and her essential purity. She was able to pierce beyond the normal physical veils to see with total clarity within herself vibrant and strange things not seen by other people all their lives. This was considered as being among the *karamat*, miracles. It resulted from the coming together of the two attributes, the external and the internal (the Secret), so that her inner was united with her outer self, and the natural tendencies were annihilated and taken into the Lord's protection.

She may well have been among the true Saints, after her long dedication, worship and sincerity. Life since its beginning and to this day has brought with it the essential and the accidental – the pain and the happiness. Those who can remain pure of soul and sincere in their approach to God, become like medicine to others: a refuge and a consolation.

Contemporary civilization, however advanced in its iron materialism and science, will always remain thirsty for the cool wave of consciousness of the unknown world. The lives of the Saints and the holy offer comfort and solace for this world which has become filled with greed, estranged from real religion and careless; which rocks itself to sleep with its inventions in the face of its own bewilderment, helplessness and disbelief in God. It has, therefore, never been without those men and women who, since Rabia's time, have chosen Sufism as their avocation; nor without those who are of the Dervishes and 'of the Way', the *Tariqa* – among whom, however, have lurked impostors and the dishonourable. These, like traders in counterfeit coins, have used to their own advantage the ignorance of the illiterate and the common people. No country has ever been free from their juggling and conjuring in the name of religion. They have harmed the ethics of man and the sanctity of all he holds dear; they have distorted and deceived. But alongside them, in every nation and community, God has bestowed sincere guardians of truth, constructive thinkers who light the way of the people, both in worldly and religious affairs. They are the teachers: the balsam and the ointment to the wounded of the Earth. They are the true Saints; and Rabia was one of them. Rabia who lost herself among her captors found herself again in the shelter of her beloved Lord.

IX

RABIA'S END

Controversy surrounds the date of Rabia's birth. Historians and researchers have failed to agree, in fact, on the definitive years of her birth or death, while other authors do not touch on either. All have agreed, however, that she lived a very long life. She was named the 'Mother of Benevolence', and it was said that it was her vigils which had given her this extra span.

Ibn Khalikan, Ibn Shakir and also Ibn al-Imaad have written that the year of her death was 801 AD.

Other well-known books written by Sufis – distinguished interpreters among them – have concurred in their reports that during the last stages of her life, Rabia was inordinately ill as a result of exhaustion following her years of effort and dedication. Each time she prayed, she cried and moaned: but not from pain. When she was asked, 'Why do you cry, Oh Rabia: what is it that grieves you?' she answered: 'Alas, my pain is of the kind that cannot be cured by a physician. The only medicine for it is my seeing the Lord. It is this hope which helps me to endure this longing for him. That is my wish: to attain that very thing in the other world.'

One of her brethren insisted that she stop crying. But she replied: 'I am afraid that in an infinitesimal last moment, a voice may say: "Rabia is not worthy to be in our presence." '

Her friend and servant Abdah, who stayed with her through the long, hard days, not leaving her side, once said to her: 'My lady, forsake this solitude. Come with me so that we can contemplate the evidence and power of God.' Rabia replied: 'Rather should you enter within and contemplate the source of the power itself.' She added, 'My preoccupation is to contemplate the power wherever I may be.' She saw the evidences of God wherever she looked: she never ceased from seeing them all around her. She used to say, in her seclusion: 'My Master, through you the ones who loved you came to be near you. For your glory, the mighty whales have praised you in the vast ocean: for your sanctity and holiness the waves have crashed. For you, the darkness of the night and the light of the day have prostrated themselves. The wheeling stars, the swelling sea, the shining moon, the bright planets: everything you have made in proportion, for you are God the Almighty.'

Her body became exhausted, but her heart remained conscious and awake. She believed that the different stages of coming close to God were too fine to distinguish with the naked eye or describe by utterance of the tongue. The heart of the Sufi (the man of knowledge) is always awake to see the way and reach the stage.

Rabia ate but little during her last week of life. Although she was sick, she was constantly occupied with prayer and fasting. Often her legs collapsed, and several times she fell from fatigue and weakness. She ached in every limb; and although she agreed to take some food, it was nothing more than the minimum needed to ease her hunger. She lived on vegetables, refusing to eat meat like her devoted and spellbound companion, the ascetic Rabah al-Qaysi. She seldom left her seclusion; but if she did happen to be seen by one of her people, they would come to her asking for her prayers. Then she would lean, troubled, against a wall, saying to them: 'Who am *I*? May God have mercy on you: obey your Lord and commemorate him, for he answers the needy who call upon him.'

It is clear that she refused to allow anyone to consider her an especially blessed person. She shunned the idea and declined to coopcrate with it, fearing that it might put her under an obligation – others seeking to use her as an intermediary between themselves and God. She wanted them to struggle and seek God and perform the oblations and prayers for themselves, so that he might answer their needs direct.

When she became too frail, she no longer left her house. Her Sufi brothers and sisters came to tend her all the time; while others stood outside her door, in reverence for her piety and merit. If anyone asked her a question, she would start to weep, the tears running down over her hands and neck.

She had nothing in her small house except a Persian straw hook, about two feet long, upon which she hung her shroud, to remind her constantly of the last day. Her bed was made from sun-dried bricks; upon this she slept and prayed. The floor was covered with an old straw mat and worn-out pieces of leather. During her last few days, she stopped taking food altogether. She felt the hour of death would soon come. She entrusted her friend and servant Abdah, the daughter of Abu Shawaal, with the last task, to wrap her in the mantle she wore during her prayers, to cover her head with her black woollen veil, and asked her to speak to none about her death.

When she lay dying, a group of friends and followers were with her in the room. She said to them: 'Leave the road open . . . I will soon be gone.' So they left her, saddened, and stood at her door attentive. As she died and surrendered to her Creator, she was reciting the Testimony of Belief.

They came back inside, weeping and full of sorrow. Her friends and her neighbours hastened to prepare her funeral. Then, praying for her, they followed her to her burial place.

It is at this point that the historians and those who have written about her death and burial entered into controversy; as they had over other aspects of her life – such as her origins and kin. The facts about her death became confused with those relating to other pious women who had been named after her, and who were also ascetics. Among them was Rabia al-Shammiya of Damascus. However, the conclusion arrived at by eminent and trustworthy historians like Yaqut al-Hammudi, and the traveller Ibn Battuta, was that our Rabia of Basra was buried in her home town; and this is a logical and natural place. Of the two other tombs which bear her name, one, on the outskirts of the Holy Sanctuary in Jerusalem, is for Rabia al-Badawiya; while the second, in the suburb of Qaymariya in Damascus, is known to the local women as 'Sitty Rabia', or 'Lady Rabia'. And there are still others.

The explanation for the existence of the two similar tombs is that these pious women came after Rabia al-Adawiyya al-Basriya, and were named after her, as we today name children after relations.

In this same way both contemporary and past historians disagree as to the exact whereabouts of Lady Zaynab, daughter of the Prophet Muhammed (mercy be upon her). Some have claimed that her burial place was in Egypt. Others have decided that it was in al-Hijaz in Saudi Arabia, or on the outskirts of Damascus. Lady Zaynab has indeed a magnificent monument in each of these places and devotees go to visit them during the yearly memoriam. It is not uncommon for different countries and cities to claim to have given rest to the same prophets and saints. They seem to share the honour of the tombs; as in the case of John the Baptist, the Prophet Yahya (peace be upon him), who has a burial sanctuary both in Damascus and in Saida, Lebanon. And al-Husain son of Ali has a mosque and a memorial tomb in Cairo, close to al-Azhar the Honourable; as well as another in the Umayya Mosque in Damascus. We do not doubt that these nations shared in treasuring relics of their noble bodies, after the revolutions and tribulations, and past battles for the Faith.

But of what use is a perishable tomb in the sand, however long the ages which have passed? What matters is this: that the one who is buried survives in the hearts of the living, and in the pages of books, for age after age and generation after generation. Rabia al-Adawiyya made known the Higher Love in Sufism; she lived to radiate the purity of the spiritual Self, and to refine humanity. We find her memory immortal and glorious; as also those who came after her, the Adept pupils of the Sufis and men of knowledge.

Rabia realized an ideal: she pointed it out for the righteous and the sincere. She lived that ideal with vision and knowledge and truth. She left for women an open door that was honourable and worthy of esteem, never to be closed again. She was a woman heading the ranks of the dedicated ones. And she became their living proof both in worshipping and in loving God.